SWEET SWEETBACK'S BAADASSSSS SONG

A GUERILLA FILMMAKING MANIFESTO

MELVIN VAN PEEBLES

THUNDER'S MOUTH PRESS • NEW YORK

SWEET SWEETBACK'S BAADASSSSS SONG
A Guerilla Filmmaking Manifesto

Published by Thunder's Mouth Press
An Imprint of Avalon Publishing Group, Inc.
245 West 17th Street · 11th Floor
New York, NY 10011

AVALON
publishing group incorporated

Library of Congress Cataloging-in-Publication Data is available.

ISBN: 1-56025-633-8

Designed by Paul Paddock
Printed in the United States of America
Distributed by Publishers Group West

CONTENTS

REFLECTIONS

Preface to Second Printing   **3**

from A Revolutionary Analysis
    by Huey P. Newton   **5**

The Baadasssss Success of Melvin Van Peebles
    by Mel Gussow   **7**

Melvin Van Peebles on *Sweet Sweetback's Baadasssss Song*   **29**

Mario Van Peebles on *Baadasssss!* and His Dad   **31**

SWEET SWEETBACK'S BAADASSSSS SONG

The Idea   **59**

Shooting Script   **135**

Dialogue   **161**

Codas   **207**

This book—
like the film—
is dedicated to
all the Brothers
and Sisters
who had enough
of the Man

". . . Sire, ceci n'est pas un ode à la brutalité que l'artiste aurait inventé mais un hymme sorti de la bouche de la réalité . . ."
(Incantation Traditionelle Du Moyenage)

"Sire, these lines are not a homage to brutality that the artist has invented, but a hymn from the mouth of reality . . ."
(Traditional Prologue of the Dark Ages)

REFLECTIONS

PREFACE TO SECOND PRINTING
1972

Sweet Sweetback's Baadasssss Song premiered at the Grand Circus Theatre in Detroit, Michigan on March 31st, 1971, and within five days grossed $45,534, an all-time house record. Two days later the film opened at the Coronet Theatre in Atlanta, Georgia, and in three days broke house records there. By all odds, *Sweet Sweetback's Baadasssss Song* is one of the most extraordinary box-office successes of our time. Reviewers acclaimed it as an artistic achievement in filmmaking.

Sweet Sweetback's Baadasssss Song was made by one man—who wrote, directed, edited, composed, starred in and produced the film.

How he made this film and achieved such enormous success is all in Melvin Van Peebles' journal—

a must for all those interested in filmmaking!

from A REVOLUTIONARY ANALYSIS
Huey P. Newton, 1971

The very popular movie produced and directed by Melvin Van Peebles called *Sweet Sweetback's Baadasssss Song* contains many very important messages for the entire Black community. On many levels Van Peebles is attempting to communicate some crucial ideas, and motivate us to a deeper understanding and then action based upon that understanding. He has certainly made effective use of one of the most popular forms of communication—the movie—and he is dealing in revolutionary terms. The only reason this movie is available to us with its many messages is because Black people have given their highest support. The corporate capitalist would never let such an important message be given to the community if they were not so greedy. They are so anxious to bleed us for more profits that they either ignore or fail to recognize the many ideas in the film, but because we have supported the movie with our attendance we are able to receive its message.

THE BAADASSSSS SUCCESS OF MELVIN VAN PEEBLES
Mel Gussow, 1972

His clothes look like remnants from a rummage sale: denims with barely a trace of blue, shirts that look slept in—and usually are. His hair is twisted in tight rows of braids, like a furrowed field, covered by a bright African skullcap. The bristle on his face is not a premeditated beard so much as an accidental accumulation by someone who simply does not have the time or interest to shave.

Around his neck is tattooed a circle of dots which he wears as a permanent necklace. On the left side of his neck, the circle is broken by these words in French: *"Couper sur la ligne* [cut along the dotted line]". On the right side of his neck, the line is broken by the English word "Cut" This is crossed out and above it is printed "Lynch." "That's only part of it," says Melvin Van Peebles. He unbuckles his belt, drops his trousers and indicates words tattooed on his right buttock. In Bambara, a West African warrior language, it says, *"Ni bessé."* Van Peebles translates: "If you can."

Lynch me—if you can. "That's my philosophy of life," says Melvin Van Peebles with a mischievous smile.

Melvin Van Peebles is a phenomenon. He is the first black man in show business to beat the white man at his own game. Admirers and detractors—and Van Peebles is controversial among whites and blacks alike—give him high points as promoter and businessman.

"He's a first-rate promoter," says Godfrey Cambridge, who starred in Van Peebles's movie *Watermelon Man*. "He can con anybody."

"As a businessman," says Gene Wolsk, co-producer of Van Peebles's musical play, *Aint Supposed to Die a Natural Death*, "Melvin is in a class with Jean Paul Getty and the Rockefeller family." Some critics think of him as an important and innovative artist: others think he is at best a mimic and an audience exploiter.

He has reached his position of dominance by merging his roles as artist and entrepreneur. "There may be other people," Wolsk says, "who are as good at promoting, but is there anyone else who is also a playwright, composer, director, film-maker, producer, actor, singer and novelist?" By his own description, Van Peebles is "a one-man conglomerate." "If you're gonna have a big mouth," he explains, "you gotta be buttressed." He already has a mountain of nerve and a million dollars' worth of buttress.

The key to his success, besides his talent, is in his audience, what he calls his "constituency." He has uncovered this audience, popularized its culture and broken racial barriers. The audience was always there, but until Van Peebles no one seemed to know exactly how to reach it. He proved that black could he bountiful, marginal could be mass and ethnic would sell.

His third movie, *Sweet Sweetback's Baadasssss Song*, which he wrote, directed, produced, composed music for and starred in, cost $500,000 to film and grossed around $10-million at the box office. "It made $5-million before three white people had seen it," says Van Peebles proudly.

"The real message of *Sweetback* is that we have the key to our own box office. It's the black dollars, the disenfranchised dollars, that go to see those products." The success of *Sweetback* has spawned a long line of imitators. There is now a black film industry. "There are five illegitimate sons of *Sweetback* playing right now in movie theaters on Broadway," said Van Peebles recently. He is planning *Sweet Sweetback's Baadasssss Song, Part Two*, starring, of course, Van Peebles.

This summer, Van Peebles has had two shows on Broadway, which is more than one can say for Neil Simon or David Merrick. *Aint Supposed to Die a Natural Death*, with music, lyrics and book by Van Peebles, opened last October and was the fifth longest running show on Broadway by the time it closed at the end of July. His new show, *Don't Play Us Cheap*, not only has music, lyrics and book by Van Peebles. He produced it with his own money and directed it. He has also made three record albums on which he sings (in addition to albums of his shows and movies) and has written five novels.

To the outsider, Van Peebles's career is marked by its diversity. His first novel, *A Bear for the F.B.I.*, was an almost elegiac reminiscence about a black boyhood in the Midwest. His first movie, *The Story of a Three Day Pass*, was a tender love story about a black G.I. and a French girl, a conscious attempt to make "a French movie." *Watermelon Man*, made in Hollywood but a conscious (though unsuccessful) attempt to avoid making a Hollywood-style movie, was a farce about a white bigot who wakes up one day as a black man. With its broad style, it seemed firmly rooted in television situation comedy.

Sweetback was a priapic and vicious racial chase about, says Van Peebles, "the radicalization of a stud." The plot was familiar—the innocent hounded by the authorities, forced to seek sanctuary among the lawless—but Sweetback is black, and his blackness is the reason for the film. The scenes of violence are explosively effective, the scenes of sex (of which there are many) are gamy and sometimes hilarious.

Aint Supposed to Die, his most forceful and fully conceived work, is a collage of songs, soliloquies spoken to music, and dances in which blacks—some in the most desperate circumstances—reveal their loves, fears and aspirations in homely and deeply felt poetry. The lyrics are resonant with the language of the street. A young black in jail remembers a girl named Lilly and a dance called Zampoughi—"Zam-poug-hi," the word becomes a cry of sex and liberation. A Lesbian lingers wistfully near the Women's House of Detention and calls to her friend, "Baby, is you gonna ever come back and dance with me?" The play ends with a Moms Mabley type of old woman attacking the audience with "Put a Curse on You," in which she excoriates humanity for its injustices— although many have wrongly interpreted the curse as being exclusively antiwhite.

As staged by Gilbert Moses in a ghetto setting of fire escapes and back alleys, *Aint Supposed to Die* provides an uncompromising but humane look at subjugated people. In contrast, *Don't Play Us Cheap* is a folksy, good-natured Harlem party. It makes no demands on the audience—or on its author.

The artistic quality of these two varies as widely as the

style. *Aint Supposed to Die* is superbly professional; *Don't Play Us Cheap* looks as if it was slapped together on the way home from a party. But for Van Peebles there is no contradiction: "For me all the stuff has a direct arrow. I've always used my own voice." As he sees it, each piece demonstrates his main purpose—to controvert "false black images" whites use in America "to confuse, drain and colonize our minds." As artist-entrepreneur he is embarked on a one-man reclamation project. "The first move for a disenfranchised people is a sense of self."

One result of his work is that he has given employment to blacks in many areas of the theater and movies—not only as performers but as stage managers, wardrobe mistresses, costume designers, technicians. As comedian Bill Cosby says, "Hundreds of black people are getting jobs because of Melvin's steel-like arms pushing doors open that were never opened before."

The range of criticism has been astounding. Van Peebles has been adored and derided for the same work (sometimes in the same review). Critics take him personally—some as an offense to their decency. There is no predicting where his support will come from. Two of the most ardent fans of *Sweetback* were the movie reviewers for *Cue* magazine and Huey Newton, who, in the fortnightly paper *The Black Panther*, extolled the film as a great revolutionary document. Many white critics who despised *Aint Supposed to Die*, embraced *Don't Play Us Cheap* for its warmth and friendliness, while *Jet* magazine thought the music was not black enough ("How would they know?" asked Van Peebles) and the reviewer on *The Black American*, a weekly newspaper, called the show "tripe" and reminded his readers that he was no fan of *Aint Supposed to Die.*

Van Peebles is philosophical about criticism. The good reviews don't sell tickets at his box office and the bad reviews don't damage him psychologically. "If I needed approval," he says, "I would never have done any of this. Each of the things was absolutely insane and impossible."

The truth is that for all his aggressiveness and image-building he seems an extraordinarily well-adjusted and coolly confident man. Wherever he goes, he is at home. He looks and talks like a street black ("like a field hand," his detractors say), which is how he defines his "constituency." The typical member of that constituency, he tells listeners, is "not the black that you meet, the erudite black that forms the bull—— buffer zone. Those people are just as indignant about my work as the whites are—they don't want their hole card peeped. My constituency is the guy in the street who makes up 90 percent of the black population."

Van Peebles enjoys being a man of the people—but the role is also good for business. His speech is a free-flowing mix of black slang and Broadway patois ("sweetiepie" is a favorite word). His plays and movies are his "product" which he is selling to his "constituency." "I started off as a kid selling second-hand clothes to winos—at a price they could afford," he says. "It's survival knowledge. My business acumen hasn't changed much since then."

Asked to talk about his childhood, Van Peebles refuses. "The most important factor in my life is that I'm black," he explains. "Everything else comes in such a poor fifth." He does not recognize that differences in economic, social, educational or regional background can essentially change a black man's life. Black is black. "You may not notice it, but you're still black. You've got all those problems to confront. You don't believe me? Look, give me a big party at Sardi's, then watch me trying to get a cab. After all the —— is over, you're black."

On the jacket of *A Bear for the F.B.I.*, he described himself as having "a happily bourgeois childhood," which is very close to the truth. Like the protagonist, he was born (40 years ago tomorrow) on the South Side of Chicago, the son of a tailor. Van is his middle name. "It's on the old birth certificate," he says. "I think my mother just thought it sounded aristo." Somewhere later in life, Van became part of his last name. "When I was 12, I was angry at my parents for not naming me Tarzan."

He grew up in Phoenix, Ill., a suburb of Chicago, and graduated from Thornton Township High School in 1949. After a year at West Virginia State College, he transferred to Ohio Wesleyan, graduating in 1953 with a better than B average and a B.A. in English literature. Of his adolescence, he recalls that he was considered a bratty child. "People thought it was orneriness. I have since discovered that it was self-awareness. I was trying to stand on my constitutional rights."

After college, he joined the Air Force, became a navigator, survived several threats of courtmartial and served three and one-half years. Briefly he painted in Mexico, then moved to San Francisco, where he supported his wife and two children by working as a grip-man on a cable car. He wrote the text for a picture book, *The Big Heart*, about cable cars, and when it was published in 1957, he was fired. He sued the cable-car company for discrimination.

"My record showed that I had never been late or absent. They said I was psychologically set to have a big accident. I went to the F.E.P.C. They said, did anybody call you nigger? I said no. Well, how can you call it discrimination? I looked up the firing rate at the company. It was 16 blacks to one white—for incompetence. That experience taught me that a man has the possibility of juggling statistics as he needs them."

One day he was watching a movie in the Fillmore district, "something like 'Mr. Joe's Goin' to the Big House,' in which they say, 'Will you sing?' while the lights dim and they electrocute him. I just got tired of seeing —— and I said I can do better than that." The impulse toward movie-making came not from "love, but from disgust." He knew nothing about movies.

"I made some short films. I really intended for them to be features. My first feature turned out to be 13 minutes long. It was about a kid who dove off a bridge. I never made experimental films. I've always been interested in the nitty-gritty human element."

He improvised. "I edited the film in a closet. I didn't know it was called editing. I was gluin' it together." He didn't have the money to hire someone to score his film so he did it himself, although he could not read or write music or play an instrument. To this day he composes on a kazoo. Lack of knowledge has never deterred him from anything. As he says, "What's so bad about not knowing?"

Looking back on his initial film experience, he says, "It cost me my wife, two children and my car." To help pay for the film he held three jobs at once and took in a roomer. "One day my wife said, 'What would you say if I told you I was sleeping with the roomer?' I said, 'I'd raise his rent.'"

Whether Van Peebles made that retort at the time or thought of it later, it is revealing: In pursuit of his movie career, everything else took second place. Everyone thought he was crazy—an unknown, untrained black man making movies. His Hollywood offers were limited to elevator-operator jobs. In 1959, he packed up his disintegrating household and moved to Europe. In the Netherlands on the G.I. Bill he studied astronomy and acted with the Dutch National Theater. One of his roles was as Rio Rita, the homosexual boxer, in Brendan Behan's *The Hostage*. His marriage finally broke up and he moved to Paris where he worked at a variety of tasks from singing and dancing outside of theaters to writing for French periodicals. For nine years, his average income was $600 a year. Asked how he managed to survive, he answers quickly, "Off women."

He moved in and out of affairs and apartments. "The trouble with countesses and baronesses," he says, "is that they don't have anything to do all day so they got you walking their poodles and going to cocktail parties and you can't get any work done. I always preferred working girls. They put in 10 hours a day and were tired when they got home, I had all day to write."

Van Peebles published his five novels in France, writing *A Bear for the F.B.I.* in English, the others in French.

They cover an even broader range than the films and plays. In Van Peebles's words, *A Bear for the F.B.I.* is the tale of "a good Jewish boyhood in blackface." It is his *Goodbye, Columbus*, only nicer—one might say more wholesomely American. It is about a young boy's awakening to prejudice, education and sex and his fondness for the Boy Scout life—hiking, camping, winning merit badges.

The Chinaman of the 14th District Van Peebles describes as a kind of contemporary French variation on *The Canterbury Tales*: During an electrical workers' strike, habitués of a French cafe gather around an oil lamp and each tells a story. *The True American*, which was also translated into Spanish and published in Mexico, is a picaresque comic novel about a black man and a white man who meet in hell and are involved "in a series of very Candide-Pangloss things." Bantam plans to publish it here next spring.

The Party in Harlem, inspired by an actual party Van Peebles attended in Harlem, later formed the basis for *Don't Play Us Cheap*, and *La Permission*, about black-white love in Paris became, in 1967, *The Story of a Three-Day Pass*.

Obtaining a subsidy from the French Government, he wrote the film treatment, directed it, supervised the editing, wrote half the music and took the picture to the San Francisco Film Festival as the French delegate. "That was a kick," he remembers. "Nobody believed it. 'You're the French delegate?'" The movie was a hit with the critics and Hollywood began making overtures.

One of the first things he realized on his return to the U.S. was that "black music didn't mirror the black movement forward." He began writing music and lyrics "that were indigenous to the man in the street." He made three albums, beginning with *Brer Soul*. The songs—sometimes raucous, sometimes lyrical—were about the inner lives of the dispossessed. The records, says Van Peebles, "were mostly a *succés d'estime.*" Later, they formed the basis of *Aint Supposed to Die.*

Finally, he signed a contract with Columbia Pictures to make *Watermelon Man* from a story by Herman Raucher, who later wrote *Summer of '42.* "Eighty per cent of the energy on *Watermelon Man* was not spent on the set but fighting in the corridors of power," One of the first battles was over casting. "They were looking for a white guy to play in black face. Three-quarters of the film the guy is black. I said, 'Let's have a black guy in white face.' Their reaction was, 'Is that possible?' The king can play a valet but can the valet play a king? They didn't understand the racist implication of this question." Godfrey Cambridge played the role, the first part in whiteface. Van Peebles had conflicts with the author, the producer and the actors. He rewrote the ending so that Cambridge stayed black instead of switching back to white. As Van Peebles recalls, the producer was astounded and protested: "You filmed it from a black point of view!"

Van Peebles learned several lessons from this experience. "People deal in compromise," he says. "I wasn't trying to do a consensus. I was trying to do a goddamn film. The studios have the power in Hollywood. One morning, I was shaving and I looked in the mirror and I said, 'You think you're a studio. Therefore you are a studio.'"

To produce his next picture independently, he used $70,000 he had earned making *Watermelon Man* and borrowed the rest. The film was *Sweetback*, shot on the run in

Watts, with a largely nonunion crew ("I had an agreement with the unions; you don't know black people—I don't know you") and a cast filled with amateurs. For the role of Sweetback—"a gigolo, a pimp and a stud—I needed someone who wouldn't give me a difficult time with the terrible shooting schedule, someone with enough experience who hadn't been softened by the media. Add that all up and run it through and it came out me." There was one occupational hazard. An unswerving womanizer, Van Peebles carried some of the love scenes past the point of simulation, and for his efforts contracted gonorrhea. "I applied for workmen's compensation—and got it," he insists.

He edited and scored the picture and then tried to distribute it. "Only two theaters in the entire United States would take it—a bingo house in Detroit called the Grand Circus and a little theater in Atlanta, Ga. The Grand Circus usually dug about $5,500 a week. We did $7,500 the first night." The picture set records in both theaters. With the help of Cinemation, a company that distributes films exploiting sex and violence, it turned into a blockbuster and soon was playing all across the country.

"I didn't go out expecting any support from the media," he says, "I made the film critic-proof by going for my audience." His initial appeal to that audience was in his title. Repeatedly he was urged to change it but he refused: "If I called it *The Ballad of the Indomitable Sweetback*, which would be the translation into whitese, a guy would say, 'Oh, yes, that's nice,' but if you bad enough to put *Sweet Sweetback's Baadasssss Song* up there, you don't have to tell him anything else."

His advertising was equally calculating: "My public doesn't read the *New York Times*, They listen to WWRL. What catches their attention is not some dried-up advertising. I just lay it out there like I thought of it. 'Hey, brother, you want to see where it's at? See this.'"

Most of the reviews were unfavorable. "The black media was very insulted that I didn't choose a more respectable segment of the black condition. The white media assumed that I was technically inept, that the 'master of nuance' of *Three-Day Pass* had run amok in *Sweetback*." He was accused of racism, of pandering to his audience, of insulting black women. "That charge was leveled by black men whose old ladies were digging the film."

To the complaint that the hero is a pimp, a murderer and a martyr, he says, "It's a straight, old, true story. He's defending himself on a number of occasions. He ain't no outlaw. There's no law he's obliged to respect. More black guys 'advancing on people' manage to be found with bullets in their backs. Sweetback just makes up 90 percent of the bloods on the street. Of course he's not a dentist or a U.N. delegate—I admit you that."

Did he consider having Sweetback die in the end? He bristled. "You've got to be kidding. The whole thing is I wanted them to enjoy it. I got tired of seeing black guys killed. Normally, the way the film would have ended—he would have gotten almost to the border and across a dusty road comes a little girl with a hula hoop. And here comes a big truck from the other direction. She doesn't see the truck and the truck doesn't see her. He dives, gets his legs broken and falls in a ditch. The sheriff comes over and says, 'Well, nigger, we're going to tell the judge about that and he's going to go easy on you.'"

In the film Sweetback kills cops and runs a bloody path to the border, which he crosses. On the screen, at the end, are the words: "Watch out. A baadasssss nigger is coming back to collect some dues." The audience loved every hairy minute. At one showing at the Cinerama Theater in New York, the audience reaction to the scene in which a police car is blown up was so loud that three real policemen burst into the theater from Broadway to see what had happened. "Glee is the word. You see some biddybop cat come in thinking, what is this? They forget they supposed to be cool. In drive-ins they flash their lights and blow their horns. It sounds like the Roman Colosseum."

Last year Charles Blackwell, now Van Peebles's production associate, suggested that Van Peebles's record albums might be turned into a musical. For $150,000 *Aint Supposed to Die a Natural Death* opened on Broadway at the Ethel Barrymore Theater on Oct. 20, 1971. Most of the reviews were hostile. The advance sale, say the producers, was about $9. But Van Peebles said flatly, "I ain't budgin'! We're in business. It's going to work." With his producers still dubious, he promised to guarantee losses up to $100,000 with his own money—more if necessary—to keep the show alive until he could find its audience.

He immediately went to work, taking charge of the advertising, organizing a sales force to send out publicity to every black group—church, school, fraternal, social— within 200 miles of Manhattan, soliciting orders for blocks of tickets. Prices were flexible. "We weren't turning anyone away," says Gene Wolsk. "We were dealing like pushcarts." Because of *Sweetback*, Van Peebles was anathema in some middle-class black circles and Ossie Davis was drafted as a respected emissary. By himself, and later with Van Peebles, Davis went from group to group boosting the show.

Slowly sales increased. By Christmas, *Aint Supposed to Die* was breaking even (at $24,000 a week); for several weeks it made a small profit. In January, it moved to the Ambassador. (The Shuberts wanted the Barrymore for other incoming shows, all of which flopped.) In a characteristic gesture of confidence in the face of adversity, Van Peebles decided "to declare January 'Black Solidarity Behind Aint Supposed to Die a Natural Death Month,' " and invited celebrities like Bill Cosby, Ossie Davis and Shirley Chisholm to take part in the performances. For its last seven months, the show consistently hovered around the break-even point. It did not return the hackers' investment (Van Peebles eventually sank $85,000 into the show) but the planned nationwide tour next season and the projected movie sale should convert it into a financial success. Meanwhile, it paid salaries—most of them to blacks—and made reputations.

It also made converts. Looking back, Van Peebles says. "It would have been nice if the reviews had been good because that would have given me the white audience, which would have acted as a cushion until the black audience came. But it didn't matter. Clive Who? Douglas What's What? Richard Whom? Instead, the black audience acted as a cushion until the whites started to come.

"I learned a lot of things about Broadway, I learned that it is underfinanced"—which is why shows close before they can find an audience. "It isn't geared at all to black-audience ticket buying. They don't do a lot of mail orders. Joan Baez will sell out three months in advance. James Brown will sell 40 per cent to 60 per cent of his tickets the night of the concert. But he will still sell out." Many of the tickets to *Aint Supposed to Die* were sold the night of the performance.

Last spring, with *Aint Supposed to Die* finally established, Van Peebles decided to stage another musical—*Don't Play Us Cheap*—despite the fact that no one in his right mind would open a musical on Broadway so late in the season. But Van Peebles is never one to respect precedent. With typical show-business heresy, he even filmed the production in New Mexico prior to the Broadway opening (the film version will be released in the fall). In financing the show with his own money (earnings from *Sweetback*), he also violated the producers' rules of order: "One of the dictums in the business is never use your own money. What fascinates me is how many people abdicate their artistic autonomy in lieu of doing it themselves."

He did everything himself, from casting the show (largely with unknowns) to directing—the first time he had staged a show. The musical opened at the Barrymore on May 16 and Van Peebles disarmed the critics. Those who had hated him now loved him. But in the beginning, business for *Don't Play Us Cheap* was even slower than it had been for *Aint Supposed to Die.* Again the show should have closed, but Van Peebles, even with his own money in jeopardy, was unperturbed. He simply doubled his efforts, used one show to push the other—and gradually grosses began to climb.

Van Peebles's office is adjacent to the office of Emanuel Azenberg and Gene Wolsk, both co-producers of *Aint Supposed to Die* and general managers of *Don't Play Us Cheap*. A disarray of posters and handbills, it has the earmarks of a campaign storefront. Van Peebles's workday usually begins at 8 A.M. and ends at midnight, or later. Often he spends the night sleeping on a couch in the office (washing out his underwear and leaving it to dry in his producers' bathroom). He rents a loft in Manhattan where he stores a few possessions, which include a long leather coat—his single concession to his newly acquired wealth. Otherwise he looks, dresses and lives exactly as he did before he achieved success. He also has an office in Los Angeles, with another couch there for sleeping. He has few close friends and considers himself a recluse.

Asked what he does with his money, he smiles and says, "I'm not into the business for the money. I'm into the money for the business." This is a favorite refrain, and there is no reason to be skeptical about it. Money for him means artistic and commercial freedom.

At 8 A.M. on a recent morning, a knock at his office door is answered by a loud voice: "Nobody here!" The door is opened and there is Van Peebles, looking tired after only three hour's sleep, it has been a back-breaking night, cutting records of *Don't Play Us Cheap*. Work began at 10 P.M. and ended at 5 A.M. After a Spartan breakfast he returns to the office full of his usual boundless energy to begin a morning filled with phone calls, meetings and decisions. He talks with a man who is trying to persuade him to sell souvenir programs of his shows. He confers in French with the woman who is helping to translate into English the novel from which *Don't Play Us Cheap* was made.

His personal secretary, Catherine Cook, comes in and he gives her a hug, a gesture repeated with almost every woman who enters the office.

He asks her for a copy of the newest issue of *Jet* and reads from it: "Black films—boom or bust. By commercial standards *Shaft* . . . hard-living, fast-loving . . . played with spirit and spunk by ex-college football star Richard Roundtree, is the all-time black-is-beautiful film. By the same economic standards, *Nothing But a Man* . . . is not beautiful at all. Again by commercial standards, black filmmaker Melvin Van Peebles's uproarious and controversially explosive *Sweet Sweetback's Baadasssss Song*, which reportedly grossed near $10-million with huge chunks of the profits remaining in Van Peebles's pockets, is also very lovely and beautiful . . . !"

He puts *Jet* down, and says angrily, "*Shaft* and *Nothing But a Man* are white films, studio films, but when they talk about *Sweetback*, 'huge chunks' remain in my pockets. The whole significance is that *Sweetback* was done with third-world technicians. It has enabled the start of this whole empire. It wouldn't have been possible under the auspices of MGM. Roundtree didn't make $12,000 on *Shaft* and they're still bragging about *Shaft* as a black moneymaker." He seems as annoyed with *Jet* as he is with MGM, "*Jet* is black-owned, or, owned by people with tinted skin. That doesn't make it black."

Then he starts talking about "media resistance" to Van Peebles, the "blackout" of him and his shows in the press and in network television, "I've had parallel publicity and advertising circuits," which have given him "a grassroots constituency." He talks about standing outside the theater handing out leaflets. "I had one old lady come back and say, 'I brought four more.' That lady brings four, then eight more will come. I had a group from the Ebenezer Baptist Church. 'Hey, folks, enjoy that? Here's another product.' The Bar Association came. I didn't know what it was. It was the Bar*maids* Association of Brooklyn and Bronx. They said, 'Could we have cocktails?' They brought their own glasses. Those are the people. That's my constituency.

"I'm trying to provide them with a sense of self. Look, Jesus Christ was white. Santa Claus was white. Ralph Bunche was white. You never saw anybody that you could say, that's me. You don't realize what that can spark in kids who've never been able to see themselves. Or never heard *their* language being talked. This legitimatizes them in their own minds. They become somebody.

"My constituency can come in to *Don't Play Us Cheap* and they don't, feel intimidated. 'That's me, man. I've been to the party.' It is *very* different from Amos and Andy. These people have their dignity. They aren't stumblebums or petty crooks. The show doesn't laugh at their blackness. I'm trying to recapture our humorous images. You can have humor with dignity. It doesn't have to be eye-rolling and massa-dis. I love those Saturday night parties. People love 'em too, but they feel guilty about loving 'em. There is a certain inarticulate sense of inferiority many blacks feel about many things very indigenous to them. I don't see any reason for not enjoying your watermelon in white company."

Asked if Broadway ticket prices aren't too high for his constituency. Van Peebles answers: "That's a white liberal syndrome. Do you know what the *Shaft* record album costs, what the Muhammad Ali–Joe Frazier fight costs, what it costs to go to the Copa? We have the cheapest seats on Broadway."

The phone rings. It is a black theater owner in Portland, Ore., who wants to know when the movie of *Don't Play Us Cheap* is coming out. Van Peebles reaches for the phone. "Hey, how ya doin'? This is Melvin. That's me, man. . . . I haven't even begun to edit it. Write me in September. Right on, brother. Hey, man—no sweat." He hangs up the phone and says, "Cats are mumbling and groaning, but the little people on the street are calling in."

At the Ethel Barrymore Theater, he checks backstage, banters with the cast, then walks down 47th Street, repeatedly stopped by friends, associates, admirers. He walks into the Gaiety Restaurant and Delicatessen. It is like Tennessee Williams going into Sardi's. The hostess greets him affectionately. He sees the Shubert business family sitting in the back of the restaurant. He walks over to them, says hello, sits down chummily at their table. "Melvin, you're a one-man dynamo," says Gerald Schoenfeld, the Shubert attorney.

Later, in a booth, Van Peebles says to the waitress, "I would like a nosh of brisket. Tell him. He knows it's for me. For Melvin. I like it with fat. I like the cheaper cuts of the brisket." A piece of fatty brisket arrives. He admires it. "That's got character. I'm not a great fan of straight meats. I like the bone and the gristle. Filet mignon, forget it. Those nice, terrible, greasy restaurants—I love them." With great relish he eats the brisket. How is his health? "Fine. Don't smoke, drink, chew, fool with girls that do."

Wednesday matinee at *Don't Play Us Cheap*. It is 2:10 and the theater is almost empty. The curtain is being held. A bus caravan is due and it is late. Van Peebles casually settles himself in the back row. Nobody seems impatient. Suddenly the buses arrive and young people, all of them black, walk down the aisle, snapping their fingers, looking shiftily from side to side. They sit down, almost filling the entire orchestra.

"These are kids who have never been in the theater before," says Van Peebles. At 2:17 the house lights go down, the stage lights go on. The play begins with a man-size rat emerging from a hole in the wall. He is soon joined by a slightly smaller cockroach and the two of them sing, "Just Don't Make No Sense." Van Peebles talks on the telephone to his sound engineer. "Bring the two back speakers up. Give me more on the right. Give me a left." He adjusts his sound until he has it exactly as he wants. Laughter and applause. Excitement builds. By the time that George (Ooppee) McGurn sings "Quittin' Time," the audience is having a party.

In a small dressing room high above the theater, Van Peebles sits at a dressing table. "People assume I'm trying to copy traditional and make a bad copy," he says. " 'Different' when it happens to come from black Americans is not considered different. It's considered a mistake. If I was from Pakistan or China, they would say, maybe there's something that we don't know, maybe he's expressing something indigenous to his culture."

Does he see himself as a revolutionary? "In this milieu, survival puts you immediately in confrontation with politics. I don't really talk about these things. Everything is in enemy territory," He denies that his reluctance to talk about politics expresses his timidity. "It has nothing to do with being timid. It has to do with winning. You don't call a general timid if he doesn't give you the battle plans for a march."

He refuses to disclose his battle plans, but suggests: "The artistic and sometimes the political and sociological ambitiousness of the product varies in direct ratio to the amount of clout I have."

Now that he has enormous clout, what will he do next? "I can't say because I don't want to intimidate me. There are so many things I'd like to do. Working on a product from one end to another takes about a year every time. After each one of these things, there's a big council meeting inside my head. The council is convening these days. Everyone is screaming, 'Me next!'"

MEL GUSSOW is a cultural writer for the *New York Times*. He is the author of the biography *Edward Albee: A Singular Journey* and books on Harold Pinter, Tom Stoppard, Samuel Beckett, and Arthur Miller.

SWEET SWEETBACK'S BAADASSSSS SONG

A quarter of a century later my movie *Sweet Sweetback's Baadasssss Song* is often lauded as being a ground-breaking achievement and my 100 percent ownership as being an astute financial move. The facts are: I didn't have partners because no one would come in with me; and I didn't do it for money in the first place. I made the picture because I was tired of taking the Man's crap and of having him define who we were to us. Sick and tired of watching the parade of jigaboos, valets and tap-dancing cooks on the big screen, I felt we had the right to define who we were ourselves. I am most proud of the fact that I decided to do something about it.

The first step as I saw it was actually a dual one. To create a commercially feasible vehicle, our society being capitalistic and all that, plus to do something that wasn't Uncle-Tommy. We were cornered, and a cornered animal should fight for survival. Like F. Douglass always said, ". . . A Slave Ain't Supposed To Die a Natural Death." Trapped in a psychological cage from childhood—a cage that says "NO, you can't"—some managed to escape; some by oversight on the Man's part, some by luck, or, by a personality quirk. But often, unfortunately when they do succeed, they go around proclaiming that bars do not exist at all.

Anyway, *Sweetback* has made me a rich man. NO, not in

money, I blew that a thousand times. I am speaking of rich in contentment—the feeling that comes with the knowledge of having been instrumental in striking a blow for justice, freedom and the triumph of the individual over a stifling social system.

Yep, *Sweetback* managed to break a bar or two in what I consider to be one of the formative places, subliminally, or not so subliminally, where the cages that enslave us are formed, and where we go to understand ourselves—the movies.

BAADASSSSS! AND HIS DAD

THE BEGINNING

"How's your daddy, he still getting some?" inquired Muhammad Ali leaning in with a conspiratorial wink, his broad rugged face grinning as he scanned the set. "Do some Malcolm for me." I'd give him a taste, one of the minister's later speeches. "Brother sure could talk couldn't he?" Ali said suddenly reflective. I had first met the Champ at the premiere of my directorial debut, *New Jack City*, but never spent time with him until filming *Ali* for Columbia Pictures.

I had already directed what became a controversial film on the Black Panthers and had been struggling to assemble funding on a piece about Dr. King for months and now here I was on the well-healed *Ali* set portraying the political icon Malcolm X (El-Hajj Malik el-Shabazz). Recently it seemed I had been re-visiting roughly the same period in history each time from a different political vantage point.

I had grown up in a run n' gun "do for self" indie film family; on *Ali*, I was like a poor kid in a candy store. With a budget, I mean a real big ass studio film, Michael Mann research budget. I visited prisons to meet with inmates who had converted to Islam while incarcerated and a car and driver took me there. Any books I requested usually appeared the next day. I met with Warith Deen Muhammad, Elijah Muhammad's son who had taken over the nation of Islam, Mike Wallace, Minister Farrakhan and Ms. Shabazz, Malcolm's eldest daughter, who was instrumental, giving me permission to humanize Malcolm as a father.

One of the last stops on my research pilgrimage was with my own dad, who it turns out interviewed Malcolm at length when he was in Paris. Malcolm had said some disturbing things and the article was never published, some believe at the insistence of the U.S. State Department. Shortly thereafter he returned to New York where he was assassinated.

Melvin Van Peebles is many things at once—renaissance man, hustler, revolutionary, wise old sage, player, father, grandfather, friend, comrade, dramatist—and he's layered like that proverbial onion revealing knowledge only on a "need to know" basis depending on your level and interest. I never knew the motherfucker got to interview Malcolm X. And here he was taking his sweet time about revealing the contents of said discussion. A pause for the revolutionary cause as he savored his stogie reflectively.

I grinned slightly at my own annoyance not too much of course or he'd notice and we'd get way off on some tangent about me letting him take his time as he saw fit. After all it was I who was once again the askee.

Anyway like I said, I'd grown accustomed to these dramatic pauses so I resorted to my usual tact, studying the lines of his hands and face. As a kid I'd often sketch out a quick cartoon of him. The jutting defiant jaw, the droop of his moustache, his heavy lids, I had him nailed. But today

I was on a mission, any move for pen or paper could result in delay.

It's interesting as a son to take a good long look at your old man, you can't help wondering if you'll end up aging like this guy. How much of you is in him? Or vice versa? Genetics? Karma? Mannerisms? Expressions? Couldn't the son of a bitch have had more hair? Well at least I didn't inherit his long graceful chick-like fingers. On some level you kind of want to keep your parents frozen in the suspended animation of your memory. I'd seen his face so many times, in so many incarnations, and yet each time some nuance seemed different, and each time, I as observer was different.

Beyond the "mortality" if he buys-the-farm-guess-who's-next-issues, "aging" is inconvenient. It complicates ones ability to place experiences. Was he different when I was a kid? Or was it simply my perspective then? Has he mellowed? Was it "tough love" or "paternal fascism?" And what about now? Can I truly grasp or articulate the complexity of all I feel about him as an adult? The dynamics have leveled out as we both grow as men and yet still we're in a constant state of flux. Especially because, unlike some fathers, the only constant with MVP is that he remains perpetually in-motion learning, reevaluating and stretching beyond any apparent comfort zone.

In his twenties he was one of the first black officers in the U.S. Air Force, then a painter, writer and SF cable car driver. Next he moved to Europe, taught himself French and became a filmmaker. In his thirties he "took the 'hood to Hollywood" with his groundbreaking film *Sweet Sweetback's Baadasssss Song* and when the studios started imitating his cinematic formula, he split for NYC. He had two plays running simultaneously on Broadway including my favorite *Ain't Supposed to Die a Natural Death*. In his late forties he started running marathons. In his fifties he became the oldest and first black trader to hit the commodities floor and wrote a book about it. In his sixties he was working on his music, directing an indie film, and getting the French Legion of Honor award. (Yeah, technically he is "Sir Melvin" now.) Now at seventy he's between Paris and New York working on two books and can still out run my ass any day.

In spite of all this and unwarranted as it may be, secretly for some time now I'd felt like my father's father. As if on some level I was his protector, played out through the role of son. I wanted to see him win, to see him get his due, his props.

I remembered his eyes the last time we almost came to blows, I was already bigger than him and pretty sure I could take him. And there he was threatening me and knowing that I probably was thinking what I was thinking, and also that I'd never want to see him lose. Maybe winning seemed more important to him on that level or to his generation of warriors. I'd never want to see that spirit broken and yet I know he's resilient enough to lose on any level and get back up; he's done it a thousand times. I don't think it's as simple as me wanting him to win, so I win by proxy or because we share a last name. Maybe I want him to remain father, at least in his own eyes. I want to see that he has achieved what he wanted in this lifetime and for him to know that he passed it on . . . we got it.

I flashed back on my own sons as little guys insisting that I was the strongest man in the world, even when I told them differently. Were my feelings about MVP some version of this?

I thought about Ali and the question he had asked, yeah at seventy my dad was still getting "some" and without much prompting he'd give you the details (too much info man). I thought about how Ali was arguably the world's first in your face "black power" athlete and that this cool old cat sitting in front of me with the dead stogie and heavy lids was arguably the world's first "black power" filmmaker. Sir Melvin Van Movies had rocked the cinematic world back on its heels with his indie revolutionary hit *Sweet Sweetback's Baadasssss Song*. Not only was it the top grossing independent hit of 1971, it was the biggest true indie up till that time.

As Ossie Davis succinctly put it, "Melvin took on the Hollywood machine on his own terms and changed the game." Not just for black film but for independent film as well. Accompanied by a pulsating soundtrack by the then relatively unknown band Earth Wind and Fire, *Sweetback* started the cinematic tradition of the empowered ghetto hero.

THE HISTORY

It's hard to comprehend the significance of what crazy Melvin did without understanding the political context in which he had to act. During the '60s, most African Americans were considering themselves "colored." The subtext of being colored was that "colored" was just slightly different from white. As if to say, "Please let us have a small

slice of the American pie. Please let us exercise our constitutional right to enroll in the same schools, sit at the same
lunch counter or even in the same movie theatre with the
rest of white America. Recognize our humanity, after all
we are like you, we're just a bit colored." During this time
the non-violent civil rights movement, spearheaded by Dr.
King was making measured gains.

Cinematically, Hollywood for years had been acting
with impunity, categorically dissing people of color. Hispanics were portrayed as oily bandits who "don't need no
stinkin' badges." Native Americans were screaming sav-
ages circling innocent white settlers who just wanted to
take the red man's land—"The only good Injun was a
dead one." Asians were deferential houseboys bowing
politely. And black folks were members of some strange
shuffling servant tribe, mumbling little more than "yes
suh," "no suh."

When America needed to get black folks involved in
World War II, Hollywood did its part by inventing what
my dad in his documentary *Classified X* refers to as the
"new Negro" or the noble "colored" character. They usually got their ass shot off in the fourth reel so the white
hero could safely escape with the girl.

I remember as a kid watching *Star Trek* and wondering
why Spock wasn't the captain of the Enterprise. He was
smarter, taller, more logical, and could clearly kick more
"Klingon ass" than Captain Kirk. From what I could
gather, Spock was the token Vulcan neo-Negro of the
future. Spock seemed to be relegated to some sort of permanent unspoken intergalactic second-class citizenship.
No matter how overqualified he was, our man Spock was

never gonna get to be captain, or get laid on the Enterprise; he like us was "colored."

Like brother Spock, Sydney Poitier, Harry Belafonte, Dorothy Dandridge, Lena Horne, and Diahann Carroll often easily outclassed their white counterparts. They were the brightest, the best we could be and yet Ms. Dandridge barred from the whites-only bathroom where she occasionally performed, had to pee in a Dixie cup. Colored audiences had to watch their new colored stars from the "colored only" section of the balcony. American apartheid was alive and well.

Brother Malcolm chuckled at us from his podium, saying it doesn't matter whether you call yourself "Negro" or "colored" or "black" or "African American" or "Christian" or "Muslim" or "Baptist," you ain't nothing but a nigger to the man. He's been whipping our collective asses for four hundred years, he's just getting better at it. Malcolm astutely went on to point out that the "Ghandiesque" turn the other cheek non-violent approach to civil rights worked in India because the East Indians were a majority and the occupying British colonialists a minority; in essence a big brown elephant sitting on a little white one. But here in the wilderness of North America, the lost tribes of stolen Africans made up a minority of 12 percent of the population.

Malcolm said you're talking non-violence to an enemy that doesn't speak non-violence, to an enemy that will beat you down while you peacefully sing "We Shall Overcome." An enemy that will sic dogs on students trying to enroll, turn fire hoses on you, jail you, lynch you, and blow up your churches.

Malcolm went on to say that you can't sing your way to freedom, power concedes nothing without demand. "Do for self." If they don't want you in their restaurants, build your own. Don't look for trouble, but don't turn the other cheek if trouble looks for you. About Ali, Malcolm remarked with his West Indian-flavored wit. "Black people need to stop singing and start swinging; Ali didn't get to be champ by singing up on freedom, he had to swing up on some freedom."

If Dr. King was the carrot, Minister Malcolm was the stick—both necessary halves of the same revolutionary coin. Dr. King had a dream that one day we'd get freedom by peaceful means, Minister Malcolm X said freedom by "any means necessary . . ." and in the end America killed them both.

The ghettoes across the United States erupted in anger and despair. The assassinations of JFK, RFK, and Medgar Evers only added fuel to the fire. Once peaceful colored folk were now getting seriously pissed off. Cassius Clay gave up his "slave name," became Muhammad Ali and refused to go kill the yellow man in Vietnam for the white man that was denying us our human rights here at home.

Folks turned their back on the Caucasian standard of beauty, no longer straightening their natural kinky hair, they grew Afros. Terrified whites fled the inner cities in droves heading for the suburbs. Movie theatres became half empty barns. Studios couldn't seem to gauge this rapidly changing audience (this was pre-multiplex). MGM was forced to sell off its back lot. Star driven flicks like Charlton Heston's *Omega Man* and *Alex in Wonderland* bombed. People who once sang "We Shall Overcome" were now singing "Say it loud, I'm Black and proud." The Black Panther Party for Self Defense rose up in Oakland in response to extreme police brutality and unemployment. The black power movement had arrived in full force, trying to fit in, and be "colored" was over. The subtext of being "black," of course, is that unlike "colored," it is the opposite of white.

Across America this incredible surge of militancy was taking place in the black community and yet Hollywood seemed oblivious. Ossie Davis had directed a black cop drama *Cotton Comes to Harlem*, and Poitier had slapped Rod Steiger back in *In The Heat of the Night*, but by and large we were still being depicted on the silver screen as servants and mammies or overqualified ubernegroes, noble coloreds trying to be accepted by the dominant culture. There was a huge gap between the explosive reality of what was happening on the streets and the surreality of what was happening on screen. What Melvin did was fill the void.

Not only did he make the first revolutionary "black power flick" but his modus operandi was revolutionary as well. It's like my father thought he was the Statue of Liberty for disenfranchised wanna-be filmmakers. Give me your tired, your hungry, your black, Hispanics, your hippies, women, and porn makers and they shall be my crew. Take all the folks who had been left out for so long, the cinematically disempowered and let them come learn to control their own imagery. Of course his goal of a fifty percent minority crew would have been an impossibility if he did *Sweetback* union, like his first studio flick *Watermelon Man*. The "good ol' boy" unions were almost exclusively male and white. Melvin took the chance of going non-union by making *Sweetback* under the guise of a black porno film. The union left smut films alone.

If you can cut off the head, the body will die. If you assassinate charismatic leaders like King and Malcolm, to some extent their movements die. The Panthers seemed to have learned that bitter lesson, rather then having one empowered leader they had several. Their slogan oddly democratic was "Power to the People." They, like King and Malcolm, were most threatening to the status quo when they crossed the color lines linking up with the Brown Barrets, (their Hispanic counterparts) or the White Radical Peace and Freedom Party. "Power to the People" meant empowering all, not only black. What Melvin did with this renegade indie film was not only empower indie filmmakers of all colors but put on screen that it was not starring a Hollywood actor but "the black community." And he dedicated it to all the brothers and sisters who have had enough of the man. All power to the people.

As Jose Garcia, my father's maverick Hispanic second unit cameraman on *Sweetback*, said, "there was a great sense of solidarity between the races back then, a sense that as young filmmakers they could somehow reach, inspire, unite and empower the masses."

The graphic images of dismembered Vietnamese children that we saw in *Life* magazine helped galvanize America's feeling against the war. The first televised presidential debates between Nixon and Kennedy in which Kennedy handled himself in a presidential manner helped swing public opinion, elect a president and change the course of a nation. The film *The Birth of a Nation* with its images of violent, lazy neo-primate darkies helped create the KKK. During the '50s and '60s the power of the media was growing exponentially. More and more it seemed that the gatekeepers of imagery and information could control public opinion and thus to some extent policy. It's easier to repress a people if you can first de-humanize and demonize them in the media. Melvin, by doing his funky angry ghetto response to four hundred years of having the man's foot in our asses, was taking that power back.

Although at age thirteen I had production assisted on *Sweetback* and played a couple roles in it—including losing my cinematic cherry—I was only peripherally aware of the slings and arrows my father was suffering during its making. He was forced to self finance, constantly on the brink of ruin, his crew got arrested and jailed, death threats, and yet he refused to submit his film to the all-white MPAA ratings board for approval. He said they're not a jury of my peers, the dominant culture has been approving negative, crippling images of people of color for years, why should they decide what our cinematic agenda should be? The film then received an X rating. My dad, true to form, printed up t-shirts that read "Rated X by an all white jury" and made it part of his marketing campaign.

At the film's completion all he had left was about $13, sight in one eye, and only two theatres in the whole United States agreed to play it. In spite of the odds, the film caught fire with the Black Panthers who embraced it as a "revolutionary masterpiece" and made it required viewing for their members. Shortly thereafter the students, Yippies, and Hippies came—the "mother country radicals" as the Panthers dubbed them.

In the end, *Sweetback* a funky black X-rated independent everyone had passed on, out-grossed *Love Story* and caught the Hollywood studios totally off guard. If they won't let you in at the bottom go in at the top. As Malcolm has said, "Do for self—don't beg for a seat at their restaurant, build your own. Melvin didn't beg to be in their movies, he shot his own. By basically self-financing MVP was his own studio. The inherent risk with "do for self cinema is personal financial ruin. He took that gamble for himself and our family and this time it paid off.

The rest is history. The studios quickly regrouped and followed suit. MGM rewrote a white cop script it had into black face and called it *Shaft*, then came *Superfly*, both with slamming soundtracks and the golden age of what would later be called "Blaxploitation" was born. As Dad often says, "the man has an Achilles pocket book."

People often ask me about the Blaxploitation era, and like other visible minorities who have on some level achieved within the Hollywood system or behind enemy lines, I find myself in that awkward position of "cinema niggerologist." I'll inevitably be at some cocktail party trying to just get my little merlot buzz on, or at some film festival often one of the few dark faces around and they'll circle in and get me. "Mario is your dad still alive?" "Didn't he do this or that?" And what's your opinion of Blaxploitation, O.J., rap music, affirmative action etc.

Sometimes the hardcore O.G. revolutionaries will pull me aside and remind me, lest I forget, that my dad's flick was truly revolutionary, because it's flawed character—by standing up against the "man"—made being a revolutionary hip. They believe that the subsequent films funded by the studios imitated the formula but diluted the revolutionary core. *Shaft* made being a cop hip, while they contended that *Superfly* was counterrevolutionary because it made being a drug dealer hip.

The more bourgeoisie despised *Sweetback* for its raw sexuality and it's in the hood portrayal of black life; to them Melvin was an overrated troublemaker and opportunist. Some believe that any flashy images of us with Afros and guns were exploitative in nature. Others, more cinema black nationalists in spirit, resent the fact that after Ossie Davis, Gordon Parks, and my dad, it was often white directors at the helm.

I suppose as I look back on it all, even if the films did eventually devolve into semi-stylish, ghetto, full-screen comic books, they did do one thing, bad or good—they did depict us as *empowered*. Even if only for two hours, we were Pam Grier or Richard Roundtree or Fred Williamson. Fuck it, celluloid escapist fantasy or not it beats the "yes suh" "no suh" tribe. At last, we too were finally Baadasssssed!

THE DEAL

The conventional wisdom in Hollywood is that audiences usually avoid biopics. Black biopics are even a tougher sell. The truth is that historically, at least here in North America when we raise our heads as brother Malcolm or Dr. King or the Panthers did, we get shot down. Hoover and his COINTELPRO cohorts did a pretty good job of wiping out our leaders and as the infamous FBI memo reads, "preventing the rise of any black messiah, anyone who might unify or electrify black people."

Traditionally we're often portrayed as victims, not as empowered. We're slaves and chauffeurs or jumping up and down hollering "show me the money" and by in large this is the type of fare the dominant culture still rewards. When they tell our story we become relegated to exotic backdrop. When Spike did *X*, he told it from Malcolm's perspective not some white reporter interviewing Malcolm. When I did *Panther*, it was their story. I didn't create a fictional white character to usher us through the narrative as suggested. Singleton did *Rosewood*, Euzhan did *Sugarcane Alley*, all historical period pieces told from our perspective. Naturally, we're at home with ourselves; we don't need a white host.

Historically most of our black towns got burnt to the ground, our heroes got assassinated or ended up broke, or broken, in jail or on drugs. Most Americans, let alone hard working Afro-Americans, don't want to work all week long to spend their ten bucks on a movie just to see themselves getting their asses whipped no matter how noble a cinematic endeavor it may be.

Ali was different, he stood up against the system, sacrificed and triumphed and Ali is still here standing. During the seventies "Black is Beautiful" era, my dad had written a line for a character in his Broadway play *Ain't Supposed to Die a Natural Death*. The line was bellowed out by actor-director Bill Duke during a surrealistic boxing match, "Black is not only beautiful it's baaad too! It's fast, classsy, asss kicking, and name-taking too!"

I turned the line over in my head while my dad sat there

in Manhattan's warm afternoon light still gathering his thoughts. It hadn't occurred to me before how much it sounded like he was writing about the champ and now the champ was asking about him. I couldn't help thinking about how much the man sitting right there in front of me had sacrificed and done. Against all odds he had triumphed and lived to brag about it.

Me
. . . Dad what do you think about me doing the
Sweetback story?

I put it right out there, interrupting the silence as if he had been privy to my inner monologue all along. No reaction, he paused then asked, mildly annoyed at the change in subject.

Melvin
A remake?

Me
No the whole period, your struggle to make it. The birth of baadasssss anti-establishment cinema. James Brown's the godfather of "soul," you're the godfather of "soul cinema." We could base it on your making of the
Sweetback book.

Pause . . . he removes the stogie from his lower lip.

Melvin
Who's *we?!*

Me
I don't know who *we* is yet.

Melvin
Well who *we* is makes a big fucking difference to me.

Me
I hear you.

He eyes me. Takes a beat.

Melvin
I love you son . . . but I don't want to get fucked on
the deal.

Me
We'd option the book, the whole nine yards, if I can't
structure a deal where I have creative and political
autonomy I won't do it. And all rights will revert back to
you . . . trust me Mel, it's just your life.

I grinned slightly, he hates that Mel shit; studio execs call
him Mel. He refused to take the bait, eying me knowingly,
a game we've played to perfection over a lifetime.

Melvin
You want to hear about Malcolm's interview or not?

Me
All ears man.

• • •

About a year later my writing partner, Dennis Haggerty, and I had written a feature film script based on MVP's making of *Sweet Sweetback's Baadasssss Song*. Eventually our film would be entitled *Baadasssss!*, spelled the same way dad spelled baadasssss, two A's and five S's.

Conceptually, I wanted our film to feel like some unseen camera crew had followed Melvin around while shooting the making of *Sweetback* and interviewing the cast and crew; our diverse ragtag "Greek chorus." I find it interesting when "good" and "bad" are not articulated, each character plays his or her own "truth" and, like life, their collective truths are often diametrically opposed.

I also wanted the film to go past the "making-of" realm and capture the intimate difficult moments, like the ones between my father and me. I wanted to get inside his head and experience the creative and political state of siege he was under at the time.

This forced me as a writer to turn the emotional chessboard around and play my father's position to the best of my ability, not just his side of the argument against what was once mine but against the world. Later when I interviewed some of the real players from the time, we were often astounded at the accuracy with which certain events had been re-created. "That's exactly what your dad said, did that mother fucker tell you that?" inquired one of his old crewmembers. And this is where things got bizarre. On *Ali*, I had experienced dreaming as Malcolm—consciously studying, immersing myself, and then being someone else twenty-four-seven until it became unconscious.

My experience on *Baadasssss!* was different. It was as if I had some paternal umbilical cord wired into my hard drive allowing me to channel directly. I'd be thinking as my father, reacting as him without ever first translating as me. I know him, have studied him, have sketched him, been taught by and fought with him long enough to know his game, his response in most situations. I soon discovered how much in fact I was similar to this man that as a kid I hadn't always liked and never consciously intended to emulate.

At any rate, Dennis and I had sent our script out to most of the studios around town and got passes, received feedback like "original," "provocative," "powerful," "unbelievable," "Is this really a true story?" "Who's the audience?" "Is this art house or mainstream?" "Black audience or white?" "Too political." "Can it be more comedy or more drama?" "And how sexy is the sex going to be, is this R?" "Can't we make Melvin more likeable?"

My dad's life was sexy, and political, and interracial, and humorous, and tragic simultaneously. To make it genre specific for the finance and marketing guys would be marginalizing some aspect of his persona. The one cat that got the script was Michael Mann—cinephile, historian, and unafraid of politically charged material. Michael Mann and his wife Summer had seen *Sweetback* on their first date.

In addition to his astute story notes, Michael, as producer, saw the inherent non-genre specific funding dilemmas we would clearly face. But he also noted another concern. He said he thought I had to play Melvin and he didn't picture anyone else directing it but me. I'm inherently familiar with the story (which is not always a positive) and I obviously had the passion for it. But doing both was a challenge. Doing both on an under the radar hardcore independent with limited time and money was a risk at best.

Flash backward a couple of weeks, Jerry Offsay was retiring as president of Showtime and producing a few one-million-dollar digital pictures. A straight shooter Jerry had expressed interest in the project. We had worked together several times over the years but I didn't see this as digital. It had to be film man—35mm, big, and a million dollars? For a period piece in L.A.?

It was Michael Mann who got me re-thinking digital. Portions of the visually lush *Ali* were done digitally and he let me get a little experience with it when I directed an episode of his series *R.H.D./LA.* The series was shot entirely digitally in L.A., often using a minimal lighting package at night.

Meanwhile the voices of my muse kept coming to me at all hours of the night. I'd wake up inspired and have to re-work some of the dialogue in the script or tighten some scene. Dennis would humor me, we'd get out the new and improved draft and still we were getting passed quicker then an Iranian hitchhiker on the New Jersey Turnpike.

Dad would call occasionally from Paris or NYC and he was cool. He knows the business and me well enough to know *no* news is *no* news and if I had news I'd tell him, so we'd just rap as father and son and leave the movie business alone.

We got other interest in the script but it was "could be, should be, might be" money. With each passing week that "no strings" million from Jerry looked better and better. My dad had a sign in his office that read "If you don't like my principles I have others." I was sliding down the slippery slope talking myself into this shit, but how could I sell it to Pops?

I hooked up with a no-nonsense line producer who did up a bare bones budget on spec. The answer came back— we could afford about eighteen days to shoot the entire film *if* and only if we paid the crew, director, and actors close to bare minimum. I knew one director and actor who'd do it for scale and not give me any shit . . . me. That solved that equation but what about everyone else? And what of old Sweetback's reaction?

Me
Hey Pop remember that offer from Jerry? (No reaction) I think I should take it while the money's still green.

Melvin
I thought we agreed that was a little tight.

Me
Yeah, yeah, it is but we'd have eighteen days . . . you shot *Sweetback* in what twenty, twenty-five?

Melvin
(Pause) Who's gonna play me?

Me
Me.

Melvin
And you're gonna direct too?

Me
Yeah man just like you did . . .

Growing enthusiasm, it's all making karmic sense to me now.

Me
We'll be doing it in the spirit of the original and we'll
even get that same fifty percent minority crew like you
had. Remember your question who is the *we* with creative control gonna be? . . . Me. The bad news is money's
tight; the good news is I can make the movie. No studio
interference—good or bad the vision will be specific.

Melvin
(Pause) Well . . . Don't make me too fucking nice.

And that was it. MVP's truncated code for have at it, do as
you will, I trust you and won't interfere. And he didn't. He
visited the set twice at my request and he saw the film only
after my final cut.

FATHER AND SON

Life seems to allow most of us the opportunity to play all
the roles. One day you're a kid dodging homework,
checking out some cute girl, the next day you're a parent
trying to get your kid focused on their homework and
your daughter's a cute girl.

My life in particular has allowed me to play out all the
roles. Yesterday I was a skinny kid with a big Afro working
on my dad's flick, the next day I'm literally playing my dad
directing me as a kid; and completing the circle, my own

children are acting in my film—three generations of the Van Peebles clan.

At times during filming it seemed surreal, wearing the same pimpified crushed velvet Sweetback outfit he wore. I'd yell "cut" as Melvin directing a scene within the film that *I* was directing, and my crew would inadvertently cut as well.

Was it coincidence that thirty years later I was subjecting myself to roughly the same slings and arrows that he had suffered? Starring, directing, producing, and writing simultaneously on an eighteen day shoot with no money to throw at the inevitable problems that would arise? Michael Mann is a smart cat and he had given me that look. That "be careful what you ask for you might just get it" look. Is this what he meant? Was this also about walking in my father's proverbial shoes to better understand him and some of the raggedy shit he did to my siblings and me as kids?

Not just the overt "wack you," or be willing to cut your 'fro off and stick you in a sex scene stuff that the world could see, but the less obvious stuff. Involving us in a battle as kids without ever explaining the war. Being unavailable as a parent to be available to fight that war. Sacrificing the opportunity cost of being our father, choosing to lead the troops in the cinematic revolution instead of playing with us, tickling us, taking us to jiu jitsu, or soccer, or movies and family adventures like I do with my kids. Giving us enough straight up "fun love" so that the inevitable and needed "tough love" would make emotional sense.

I feel sorry for my father on that level because he missed out on the early years with us, the pure irreplaceable "snuzzle" love years that I savor with my brood. Having missed them he has no real idea what he missed. Now having said that I had gone over my list of "father/son grievances" with my dad years ago and he listened respectfully. Agreed and apologized in some cases, and not in others, and even more disturbing, as many parents (myself included) didn't always remember some shit that was momentous to me. He handled it well, may I be as graceful as he. I believe I forgave him. I also know that on some level my kids will perceive me as letting them down, they may in turn compensate with their children giving them what they lacked from me and so on. I only hope that the desire and ability to communicate our differences is there as it has been with me and the old man.

Don't get me wrong, I know I've been blessed with the parents I needed. "Not always getting what you want" as the Stones sang, but surely I got what I needed. Both my folks are exceptionally cool avant-garde individuals who have made living and thinking outside the box an art form. They were a young, artistic, hip, non-materialistic, interracial, and politically engaged couple.

After traveling Bohemian-style through Mexico and Amsterdam, my folks divorced. My sister Megan and I came back with our mother Maria to settle in San Francisco during the not always so peaceful peace movement. Dad stayed in France building up his cache as a French filmmaker. I didn't really get to know the man until the summer of 1970. I was about twelve and he had moved back to the States, rented a one-bedroom flat in Hollywood, and started making *Sweet Sweetback's Baadasssss Song*.

Someone once said maybe it's the mother that shows you the mountain, and the father that teaches you how to climb it. My mother had shown me the mountain so to speak. She turned me onto the arts, ecology, peaceful protest, Altamont, The Grateful Dead, Bob Dylan, Haight-Ashbury, and the zen of mat surfing. A free spirit who dabbled in photography, Mom encouraged my creativity. It was Mom who worked with me on every audition, making sure I got the nuances and lines right.

If Mom had shown me the mountain, Dad taught me how to climb it, i.e. make a living doing what I love. *Sweetback* was film school for many of Dad's non-union crew, I was no exception. While other kids were out playing or at camp, I was organizing props, sorting filmstrips, storyboarding, or going for coffee. In reality, I was probably a hell of a lot less useful than Dad led me to believe. But you see that's MVP's trick, the "love" part of his "tough love" regimen. The man encourages that "I know I can" sense of self work-ethic thing—"empowerment." As Granddad had always said, "Can't be afraid of hard work." My dad taught me to survive.

Forget whether or not I'm the guy's son, only a dozen people care about that. I'd always felt this was a great story period. David vs. Goliath, a man with a vision and a Malcolm "do for self" spirit. As Bill Cosby put it, "Melvin had a dream, woke up, did it, and it's still good." But whatever my own personal motivations might have been or not, I had a choice, make the film under less than ideal conditions or postpone it indefinitely. I felt it was time, I wanted to do Dad's story while he was still around to see it. The very fact that I could do the film under less politically

adverse conditions then when he did *Sweetback* was a tes-
tament to his sacrifice—he had kicked the Hollywood
door open. In all likelihood, had he been the cuddly, ever-
present dad I might have wanted I wouldn't be here now
enjoying the freedom I have as a filmmaker. The dominant
culture would still have a strangle hold of our imagery.
We'd still be the supporting cast, one-dimensional vil-
lains, or grinning and clowning as we assist the white
leads. I'm not saying that we are not that now but we're
not that exclusively.

The black power movement paved the way for the
women's movement, the gay rights movement, Latino,
Asian and other movements. What Melvin did was show
us and the establishment that it was possible to have an
independent vision that made a pile of money and that
there was a big ass black and alternative audience out there
to be reckoned with. That's powerful stuff and it reverber-
ated beyond race and class lines throughout the film community as a whole.

Of course the tight shooting schedule on *Baadasssss!*
kicked me and the crews collective asses, but in a "Niet-
zsche" kind of way, "That which doesn't kill you makes
you stronger." In fact I believe my role as filmmaker on
a fierce independent playing a filmmaker on a more
fierce independent was served by the intense pressures
we faced. There were brakes between lighting set-ups for
the other actors but not for me. I was forced to remain
in an intense, ever-alert, pro-active mode reminiscent of
my dad. Always in the moment, strategizing, planning
the next shot, the next day, dealing with the fire mar-
shals, the actor that flaked, no permits, unions, MPAA,

anticipating the next crisis—and in this storm I found him. I found something central to my dad's character, his ability, his sheer will to get it done, with humor, with force, by any means necessary.

With no time to act I just was. In the end I made no attempt to play him as good guy or bad guy, I played him as I felt him, as I knew him. The truth.

SWEET SWEETBACK'S BAADASSSSS SONG

THE IDEA

February 1970 I'm driving north along a highway looking for a place to turn off into the Mojave. I have this idea about communing with myself in the bosom of the wilderness, proving once again that we are part, at least in part, of all that we were programmed to dance to even way back in good old Sunday school—right—but anyway for the last thirty miles or so, ever since I had hit the "real" desert (or what looked "real" to me having never been to the desert before legit or otherwise my expertise coming from—you guessed it) the western wilderness of our pioneer forefathers et cetera had been fenced off with barbed wire on both sides of the road with a warning posted at regular intervals saying NO TRESPASSING AIR FORCE GUNNERY RANGE, or something like that. From time to time there would be a gate, but I let it slide by, I could just see myself getting strafed in mid-meditation. Finally the gunnery range on the left-hand side ended, but I drove on to give myself kentucky-windage against super-piss-poor shots.

AHA—a road. I turned off the highway. Right away, the road dwindled into just a trail leading over a little hill. I drive over the rise and there I am in the real desert, sandwise and solitude-wise just like I always imagined it would be. The only thing breaking the sky-meeting-desert horizon was electricity in the form of an endless row of huge pylons carrying wires. I gravitated towards the pylons, being from the city, and parked the car in a little dip. I got out of the car and squatted down facing the sun. I unbuttoned my fly, leaned back against the front fender of the car getting myself comfortable, and pulled out my pecker and began to beat my meat. I was on a mission.

Something was troubling me, some idea was lurking back there in my mind waiting for the coast to clear to be born. That's what I was trying to do with the sun in my face and my prick in my hand, trying to clear my stage, trying to take a shortcut to Purityville so that whatever it was would come out and rap to me. I knew me well enough to realize that I would probably end up going along with the lurking blob back there and I hoped it was at least something I approved of.

I used to not get along with me because the ME I WANTED TO BELIEVE I WAS was always battling the ME I REALLY WAS. The REALLY WAS always won, naturally, but not before a great deal of time and energy had passed under the old bridge and reams of tension and tape and general bullshit had constipated and polluted me around. Anyway, one day I figured out "Shit," in the name of efficiency, if nothing else, why don't I just do from the start what I am going to end up doing in the end anyway. It sounds simple as can be and maybe for everybody else it is.

When the ME I WANTED TO BELIEVE I WAS was running the show, it vacillated, procrastinated and the destination was always out of focus and goals were usually changed in mid-stream, whereas the ME I REALLY WAS was clear-eyed, firm-treaded straight as an arrow and level-headed and could always explain concisely and precisely what the ME I WANTED TO BELIEVE was doing wrong. Of course being a guilty bystander of the modern western deification of the "NATURAL," I attributed all my wishy-washy woes and general fuzzy bullshit to the fact that the REAL ME was not at the helm. Anyway, to-make-a-long-story-short, despite Herculean difficulties, I finally managed to install the REAL ME in power. Things improved, but just a little bit nowheres near the sharp Jack Armstrong-cum-Horatio Alger bulls-eye type progress I had projected. In fact when the REAL ME I just knew was infallible gained control, its clear eyes began to glaze and its firm tread began to wobble and hyperbole continued to be the order of the day. Maybe the REAL ME had been held in second position so long it had a guilt complex about leading or something.

So I came up with this distilling program. I would decide what I wanted and analyze how to get there with as much dispassion, distance and intelligence I could muster up. Not only did this help me check out my motives and organize my thoughts, it provided me with a yardstick to judge myself with on the way and it provided me with a beam to stay on course once I had stepped into the forest, leaped into the soup.

I called this my UP-FRONT AIMS PROGRAM; the name wasn't lyricism itself maybe, but the program worked.

Normally when I felt some milestone or other coming on, I would hibernate for a few days or weeks, however long it took, until my spirit was clean enough for my muse's taste. Then my muse would come out and introduce the project or whatever. (Then if the idea passed my inspection, more or less a formality—it always passed, I

had the veto power but was afraid to use it—I would give
it my up-front aims program processing.)

I was in a time bind so I was trying this new experimental crash method. I called it semen-shock. Maybe I
could have brought a girl or a couple of girls with me to
ball but that would have meant dividing my attention.
That's why I decided on using my good old childhood,
Mrs. Thumbs-and-her-four-daughters method. Intellectu-
ally you see, it all made sense but just like years ago, intel-
lectually or not, I was ashamed of getting caught AT IT. I
was even ashamed of having the phone ring while I was
doing IT. Even if I didn't answer it, I KNEW they would
KNOW. Anyway, to make a long story short, that's what
and why I was behind a dune, crouched down by the car
pounding away at my joint.

Anyway, what am I apologizing for, they have electro-
shock, so why not semen-shock. I even saw this jive-ass
movie once where the doctor used racial-shock. This negro
soldier had a traumatic war experience and couldn't walk
and the doctor couldn't find anything wrong so in the
film's big scene the white doctor calls him a BLACK (a big
NO NO at the time) dumb nigger coward and veins stand
out on the brother's noble colored features and he strug-
gles to rise! . . . He stands! . . . (Look he's standing . . . Oh
look he's so angry he doesn't even notice) . . . The brother
makes a faltering pace toward the doctor, then another . . .
You're walking, the doctor says . . . The brother realizes he
is walking and collapses with joy and is caught by the Great
White Father once again. (Completely unrealistic because
as Uncle Tommy as that nigger had been, he wouldn't have
raised his hand to a white man to even save his own

Mammy.) Then the doctor apologizes and tells him that he wouldn't really call him nigger except that that was the only way to get him better fast and that there was a war on and that they were short of beds and besides they were all Americans and that the country was beginning to realize what a great contribution its colored folks, etc.

Yum-yum (pound, pound) yum-yum (pound) oh heavenly (pound). Goddamn, just THEN my muse announced it was ready to escort the idea forward.

Here I am, it said, cool it, brother, I said. (It seems my semen scheme was succeeding but I was too heavily occupied to get into it.)

Yum-yum (pound, change hands, pound). Yum—I'll be right with you—yum. Amen-yum. My muse copped an attitude, you suppose to be trying to get in touch with me . . . I'm your reason for being here. Yeah, yum, right (pound, pound) yum-yum, with you.

WHAM, SHAZAM, I leaned forward automatically (with the experience that comes from years of turning my brain matter gray and growing hairs in my palms) to keep from soiling my pants.

My first thought was that the entire thing had been a set-up to rationalize my beating my meat and that I was pretty Goddamn old to be out in the sand and sagebrush masturbating. Then I realized that it had worked after all—that the muse had rolled the stone away from the cave. I peered into me and saw I was tired of the Man (this was new, already?) but there was more. I was going to do my OWN movie.

My ME I WANTED TO BELIEVE I WAS (or maybe it WAS ME) starts right in on its sabotage trying to talk me out of it. Who do you think you are, a big film?

Yes, a big film.

You don't look much like a director to me, let alone a producer, standing there with your fly all open. (I zipped up my pants.)

What about the story?

No problem, I got an idea (I lied).

What idea?

A brother . . . A brother getting it all together, you dig . . . and no cop out.

What about bread if it's going to be such a big film? . . . And what do you know about producing, mother fucker?

A producer produces, mother fucker.

I was walking through the desert. I turned at the top of a mound. The car was tiny in the distance.

I'll get the bread, I'll get it, I told me.

How about the Unions hassling you?

I'll have tight security, what they don't know won't hurt me.

I didn't let myself get intimidated either . . . I'm going to have fifty per cent of the folks on the crew too . . . I was really getting into the thing . . . Guerilla Cinema. The idea seemed like it had always existed. I drove back to L.A. It all made sense, in ghetto-wise theory, anyway.

When I did *Watermelon Man*, I had gotten a brother into the producing end. I figured that it would be out of sight if I could pick up the bread from the get-go even before I wrote the script. Usually all the producing cats went around trying to put super high-priced deals together, "packaging" as they call it:

> "I'll get such and such a star use L as the director
> he'll be hot right after this new one comes out a

smash baby my friend knows the prop man and he said the crew stayed in stitches anyway I've got a writer one of the biggest who wants to do the screenplay he'll work on spec he's so excited about the treatment he was playing tennis with Ralphie and he dropped him a hint and he's begging me to let him take it to the front office now . . . (Ad infinitum) . . ."

That's packaging, baby.

I went to see the brother and we power-hand-shaked each other for a half hour and did how-you-doing-my-man and same-old-same-old to each other for another half hour then finally got down to it. I told him about the film and asked him for financing suggestions.

Sure he could help me he knew this actress and she had a friend at the front office of Warner's and with his music connections plus he was going to play tennis with J.D. and he would drop him a hint and he'd be begging to let him take it to the front office . . . etc.

O.K., so you can't win them all, anyway, it was a long shot.

First things first. And the first thing was the script. What did I want to accomplish script-wise? I wanted to take another step in getting the Man's foot out of my ass.

Actually I knew the answer to that question before I asked it. But I wanted to fulfill fully the questionnaire part of my UP-FRONT AIMS PROGRAM. To get the Man's foot out of my ass means to me logically to get the Man's foot out of all our black asses. This seems to me an apparent truth, but many of the buszwazee brothers don't seem to realize it. They don't seem to understand that they are not free as long as their other brothers are still in slavery. (If they would get out of some of those limousines once in a while and even try and catch a cab or two, the truth would come home to them very rapidly.)

Anyway next step, how specifically to get the Man's foot out of our ass. The first beachhead, the very first thing that we must do is to reconquer our own minds. The biggest obstacle to the Black revolution in America is our conditioned susceptibility to the white man's program. In short, the fact is that the white man has colonized our minds. We've been violated, confused and drained by this colonization and from this brutal, calculated geno-cide, the most effective and vicious racism has grown, and it is with this starting point in mind and the intention to reverse the process that I went into cinema in the first fucking place.

"Where is Brer?" I asked me, he was digging TV, movies and the sounds. But TV was out; television at this stage of the game, as it is practiced in America at least, is not a fea-sible tool for carrying really relevant ideas to the minds of the disenfranchised. The umbilical cord from the TV pro-gram to its sponsor is short and very vital and can be cut abruptly, too abruptly for a program to get away with pushing any extra-uppity ideas. Each thing must be self-contained breadwise. Artistically, we must be guerilla units too. Each project must be a self-contained unit, otherwise it will be subject to the inevitable slings and arrows of out-rageous racist economic pressures.

Anyway story-wise, I came up with an idea, why not the direct approach. Since what I want is the Man's foot out of our collective asses, why not make the film about a brother *getting* the Man's foot out of his ass. That was going to be the thing.

Now to avoid putting myself into a corner and writing something that I wouldn't be able to shoot, I made a list of the givens in the situation and tried to take those givens and juggle them into the final scenario.

GIVEN:
1. NO COP OUT.
   A. I wanted a victorious film. A film where niggers could walk out standing tall instead of avoiding each other's eyes, looking once again like they'd had it.
2. MUST LOOK AS GOOD AS ANYTHING CHUCK EVER DID.
   Very delicate point. One of the problems faced by a black filmmaker (in fact any American independent filmmaker who wants to produce his own feature, just more so for a brother) is that Hollywood polishes its product with such a great deal of slickness and expensive perfection that it ups the ante. That is, if I made a film in black and white with poor sound, even if it had all the revolutionary and even story elements that anyone could hope it would have, brother would come out saying, well, shit, niggers can't do anything right. I saw

such and such a film in color and 35 mm and so on and so on, how come we have to make such rinky-dink stuff. Not realizing of course that the price of freedom is often poverty of means. Well I felt that this problem was a little too involved to attack, so I was determined that the film was going to look as good as anything one of the major studios could turn out.)

3.   ENTERTAINMENT-WISE, A MOTHER FUCKER. (I had no illusion about the attention level of people brain-washed to triviality.)

  A. The film simply couldn't be a didactic discourse which would end up playing (if I could find a distributor) to an empty theater except for ten or twenty aware brothers who would pat me on the back and say it tells it like it is.

  B. If Brer is bored, he's bored. One of the problems we must face squarely is that to attract the mass we have to produce work that not only instructs but entertains.

  C. It must be able to sustain itself as a viable commercial product or there is no power base. The Man has an Achilles pocket and he might go along with you if at least there is some bread in it for him. But he ain't about to go carrying no messages for you, especially a relevant one, for free.

4.   A LIVING WORKSHOP.

  A. I wanted 50 percent of my shooting crew to be third world people. (This could conflict with point 2 if a script was not developed extremely carefully.) So at best a staggering amount of my crew would be relatively inexperienced. Specifically, this meant that any type of film requiring an enormous technical sophistication at the shooting stage should not be attempted.

5. BREAD.
   A. SHORT! SHORT! SHORT!
   B. Normal financing channels probably closed.

6. MONKEY WRENCHING.
   A. I would have to expect a great deal of animosity from the film media (white in the first place and right wing in the second) at all levels of filmmaking. (I would have to double check my flanks at all times and not expose myself to the possibility of racism, in everything from keeping tight security about the 'real' script to choosing locations to dealing with the labs and perhaps a portion of the cast and crew too. As costly as it would be, I felt I would have to leave myself a security margin.)

7. UNKNOWNS AND VARIABLES.
   A. CALIBER OF ACTORS.
   B. CALIBER OF CREW.
      I would have to write a flexible script where emphasis could be shifted. In short, stay loose.

I suppose I could have made an infinite list of liabilities and assets, especially liabilities . . . but anyway.

(ASSET 1.) I kept asking myself what could I do that Hollywood major studios couldn't. The thing that kept occurring to me was that I could delve into the black community as they would never be able to do because of their cumbersome technology and their lack of empathy.

(POSSIBILITY 1.) Something begins to jell. Strange how you store things. Somewhere I read an interview with this big director where the interviewer asked how he managed to get away with such audacious shots. He replied something to the effect that as long as you kept the story moving, you can put the camera anywhere you want and cut anywhere you desire. WHAMMO. I decided I would pack the scenario with enough action for three goddamn films so I would be able to get away with anything. I would even use triple or quadruple screen effects like they do to prop up television detective stories if I had to.

(OPPORTUNITY 1.) Most filmmakers look at a feature in terms of image and story or vice versa. Effects and music (most directors can't carry a tune in a fucking bucket) are strictly secondary considerations. Very few look at film with sound considered as a creative third dimension. So I calculate the scenario in such a way that sound can be used as an integral part of the film.

I would have to choose a story line strong enough to provide continuity, but simple enough to give enough room for digression without losing its directness. I approached the film like you do the cupboard when you're broke and hungry: throw in everything eatable and hope to come out on top with the seasoning, i.e., by editing.

A couple of the unknowns still bothered me. To keep this strong story line going, I felt I would have to use one actor as the principal vehicle that I could hinge other things onto. Next, I had decided to use cameos but because of the looseness of their construction, I couldn't foresee the exact running time of the film, so I devised an accordion section for the film that could be lengthened or shortened according to the time consumed by the various other parts of the script.

All this shit swarmed around and around in my head. About this time I had a burden lifted, it dawned on me that I was in charge, and whereas I usually try to impart in my work the idea of getting the Man's foot out of our ass without letting it show to the Man too soon, I did not have to do that this time. So I thought, well, why don't I then, since this could be it, why don't I make a film directly about, accent the positive, what I'm all about, what we are all about. That is, it would be the story itself of a man getting the Man's foot out of his ass that on close examination would fit the necessity of the script for a strong, action-packed storyline if it were told in that way. That's where it's at.

(TITLE) The media is a very important part of the message and that's why I called it *Sweet Sweetback's Baadasssss Song*, instead of some phony shit with a subtitle about it being made for brothers and sisters. With that title they would KNOW.

The end is all very well and good and the number one priority. However, in the meantime, if a way can be devised to make the means productive, you're that much more ahead of the game. I was trying to utilize all the potential of the film and I hoped to get double duty. Not only a film per se, but since I was using a large percentage of disenfranchised people, a self-sustaining workshop situation. When you are funded by a group, when you are not self-sufficient, if you become too relevant for the particular taste of the funding group (at any stage of the game), the Man can pull the economic rug right out from under you. So the film also had this other aspect to it. I looked at it as a workshop situation where people carry the fight onward while at the same time they're gaining the necessary technical knowledge to be even more effective in the struggle for the minds of third world people and other people of good will.

I got myself a piece of brown wrapping paper and got on the floor where I could work comfortably. I noted all the givens, unknowns, liabilities, assets and opportunities as best I could. One thing I was sure of, it was going to be done in 35 mm and in color. Sometimes I get the impression when I'm seeing a movie, that guy set out saying to himself, "Just how much bread can I waste, just how much bread can I utilize on this project?" Sometimes I get the impression that the cost of the film often has more to do with the directors' and producers' egos than with the project itself. Often they want to see how much money they can control, i.e. how much they are loved or how bright they are. Sometimes the other side of the coin is their thing—just how much the cost can be cut down and still have the public sit through 90 minutes of that particular subject. It's sort of a feast-or-famine thing.

I knew we would be very short of bread and so I tried

to judge this thing as pessimistically as possible. After devising a low-budget film, I then added touches that would only be found in the most expensive film. In other words, I tried to make a low-budget film without the low budget, but with the advantages of both.

The biggest problem looming in front of me was how I was going to get away with shooting the film with my brand-new reputation as a major film director. I knew I would be watched and the Unions could make it extremely difficult for me to make a major film. The answer was so obvious I didn't see it for a few minutes. The Unions don't trouble themselves over smut films, that is, pornographic films, which I suppose they consider beneath their dignity, and there is even an entire parallel distribution circuit for these films. So Nutsville went to cover my project and told everyone I was making a beaver film (Beaver is Californese for vagina).

Voilà. There it was on my piece of brown wrapping paper. Then I gave it to my secretary and the final draft was finished on March 6th at 6:20 P.M., 1970. I knew it was March 6th at 6:20 P.M. because I didn't use the title on the front page, not wanting to freak out the copyright people. I simply put the date. Two weeks and three days had passed since the time when I had leaned back against the car in the desert and unzipped my fly.

● ● ●

It was all set to go now except for one major little item—money. I was still under contract to Columbia for *Watermelon Man*, but I didn't have much hope that Columbia would pick up this script. I thought back to a front-office discussion I had had with them prior to my trip to the desert. We waltzed around a project known as the *Malcolm X Story*. Stanley Schneider and a number of his executives had met with me about the possibility of maybe my getting involved in the project. For one thing, I was determined not to do another film with a Hollywood producer riding on my back as co-director, and the film already had a producer. But most of all, I refused to do any black-oriented project without having the final say-so on it and naturally the studio wanted final cut. (I sort of had final cut on *Watermelon Man* by simply breaking my word and not shooting a disputed scene the two ways we had agreed on, the way they wanted it and the way I wanted it—". . . and then we will [pat-pat] see later, Mel . . .")

Another straw that broke the camel's back and drove my agent practically to tears (I still had an agent at the time) was my refusal to read the script for free. Now everyone at Columbia admitted that the script *was not what they wanted*. What they wanted was for me to read the script and give my ideas on it to see if I had the right approach to the Project. It seemed a little ludicrous and I told them so, that I, as a black man, would have to report to them as white and let whites pass judgment to see if I had the proper concept and outlook on another black man.

"Well, Mel," they said, "why don't you just read the script anyway and tell us what you think."

"O.K. I'll read it for 5,000 dollars."

WHAM. Raised eyebrows and the stench of shit hitting the fan filled the room.

"You're joking, Mel."

"Nope. If you want me to read it, that'll be 5,000 please."

Did I know Malcolm X . . . Have you read the Book . . . etc.

"I haven't read it, I've lived it."

"Well, we'd still *like* you to read it," they said.

"O.K., for 5,000 dollars."

"Are you serious?"

"Yes, I'm serious . . . That's my going rate as a niggerologist . . ."

There was a short, red-faced pause and that ended the discussion. Like I said, I didn't have much hope that Columbia was going to meet my terms—to produce, direct, have final cut and a 50 percent minority crew which would mean non-Union members. These were things they wouldn't get involved in. There was one outside chance that maybe they would simply give me the money under the table and let me go do my film with the understanding of their having distribution. But it was an outside chance, an outside dream rather, a long shot, but when you are sitting faced with blank pages in your typewriter and you need a *hope*, something, anything, to get you through the next page, beggars can't be choosers. I didn't believe it myself, but it was all I had. Frankly, I didn't know where to look.

I had to go to New York to check some publicity work on *Watermelon Man* and I gave the script to Stanley Schneider, and at the same time my non-negotiable, as I put it, demands for shooting.

A few days later I was given a great honor. Stanley invited me and my date to dinner. Our relationship had always been very cordial. In fact, I suspect that he had passed the order during the shooting of *Watermelon Man* that I was to be left alone as much as I was. Naturally, I didn't bring a date because they would have tried to use the occasion to "understand" me better through my choice of girls. My role in our relationship had always been to play sort of the ghetto-gamin-prodigy who kept to his uncomplicated-picturesque-ways. Neither one of us wanted a direct confrontation, so we had set up this ritual to avoid coming to grips. This way we could feel each other out.

There were nine of us at dinner, Mr. and Mrs. Schneider and three more couples and me. Unfortunately, the lady sitting directly on my right was very coquettish and a beautiful young thing. Very décolletée, and every time I would turn toward the mashed potatoes which were on my right, she would cover up her breasts, calling attention to the fact that they were pretty much uncovered in the first place. Because she was French we began to rap in French but my caution meter started burning and I glanced across the table and saw her boy friend flushing and looking a little nervous and I realized he thought his pussy was in jeopardy. I then became very interested in the architecture of the ceiling because I could get pussy in the post office and didn't want any trouble. Finally the dinner was over and while the other guests mingled around, I managed to get into the den with Stanley.

"Well Stanley, what do you think of the script?"

"Well Mel, very interesting. But we just did it . . . We would just be repeating ourselves."

"What do you mean, you just did it?"

"Well your film is about black people and the police, and we just did *Lord Byron Jones*."

Suddenly a distance like a zoom out. The room was maybe 30 feet deep but it seemed like miles and miles and miles and we were at opposite ends. I tried to explain to him that *Lord Byron Jones,* where a black man gets castrated, cut up, beat up and done in, and stands there with a bible in his eyes, wasn't the same thing *AT ALL* as *Sweetback.*

"Well, there's so much violence in this. Do we need all this violence? I'm not sure violence is the answer."

"You got violence downstairs if you let it happen," I pointed out. "But you four got six-foot guards at the door . . . Naturally you don't know from violence. What would happen if your six-foot guards weren't there?"

Right on time like a bad movie, the news broke in on the television set. We slowly walk around the den and Stanley makes a point about how black people are making progress.

"Look at that woman (pointing to the lady announcer on T.V.) she's black. That wouldn't have happened a few years ago."

I asked him when was the last time he'd been up to 125th. That lady didn't look like any niggers I knew, or sound like any of the folks I knew either.

At this stage of the game, the guests began to filter into the room. I continued my discussion with Stanley, and the other guests began to join in politely. Non-consequentially, of course, as white folks will do, after dinner and brandy. I felt a reassuring pat on my knee and I turned. It was Mrs. Schneider.

"I understand, Melvin," she said, smiling sadly. "They don't understand as well as you and I because I come from a poor family too and I know what you mean."

The shit was beginning to get a little thick, but I tried to work up some empathy for her sympathy.

"Black people live in this building and they deserve to be here . . . But you know I've always gotten along especially well with black people," she said. "We have such a good understanding, like my maid and I, for instance . . ."

I stood up and told Stanley it was coat time.

"What?" he said.

"I said coat time. Give me my coat or I got to git it."

He got up and gave me my coat and I left. Talk about burning your black bridges.

The door clicked behind Stanley. The hallway seemed quiet and politely dignified. The elevator was quiet, polite and dignified, the door man quiet, polite, dignified, gracious. All that quiet, polite dignity began to psyche me out. Was I being unnecessarily belligerent? Then I started waving my arms trying to get a cab and they kept on going. I began to laugh. There I was standing in the New York night, laughing. How the fuck would those folks know. The cabs would slow down till they got close to me and they saw I was a brother, then they stepped on the gas instead of the brake. A cab came close enough for me to catch it with my boot. I kicked the side of his door and I hoped I bent the mother fucker in half. The driver slammed on the brakes, then thought better about it and sped up again. I still didn't have the bread, but I sure felt good. Well anyway, niggers got feet and I walked on back to the hotel.

• • •

I began to look for bread in every nook and cranny, every armpit and nostril. Any and every other Goddamn where.

There were little pot-gutted rich businessmen who wanted in on the glamour and the starlet pussy, but this was not a musical comedy with acres of action. There were, as usual, the sharp-faced, squinty-eyed parasites and their cousins, the squinty-faced, sharp-eyed parasites who never have any money but who try to use any occasion to attach themselves to a film. The astonishing thing is how successful many of the squinties are. On any given film these leeches can be seen hanging off the gunwales but I didn't know them, because, thanks to my UP-FRONT AIMS PROGRAM, I had been transformed from a 90-pound, insecure weakling to a 155-pound all-American juggernaut.

Next, there were businessmen looking for non-risk investments in a high-risk field. It was at a luncheon with one of these types that all the shit fell into place. Bill Cannon, a writer-director friend of mine, invited me and another film friend of ours, Steve Schmidt, to have lunch with him and a Pigeon at Musso Franks. The topic of discussion (it was always our topic of discussion) was how to raise bread to finance projects. Bill had a plan. He felt that a united group of young filmmakers stood a better chance of floating a loan or an investment from the money people. They would feel more secure because they were getting more variety and an organization.

Next he had this idea about taking a house with working space and equipment for young writers who would be in on the project where we would all live together. "Young" is a sort of euphemism for filmmakers who haven't made two or three features. The money people would be in on the original project, but they would only be financing the preparation of the package to a major studio, "first backing" as it's known in the industry.

I told Bill that I disagreed with him on both counts. First, us banding together in a commune of filmmakers, next "packaging" in general and especially looking for backers for money to prepare packages.

"I don't want a package of stars and scripts."

"Yes, but you need to live in the meantime."

"Well, I think your method only postpones the inevitable. You still have to come up with the main bread after the package and you have yourself a partner in for a sizable chunk for no reason . . . simply because you need a father figure to lay a few dollars on you in advance. Forget it!"

"Melvin," Bill said, "I think you're wrong."

We laughed at each other and smiled. Bill is one of those rare people. Although he might have a different approach attackwise, he doesn't hold it against you if you use yours and it is successful, which is a lot scarcer in folks than I like to think about. Anyway, I had agreed to come to lunch because I was sort of the man of the moment, industry-wise, having just finished *Watermelon Man* under budget and on time. Besides, *Watermelon Man* hadn't been released and was a big hit. (In fact every film "in the can", as they call it when it's finished and before it's introduced to the box office, is a big success.)

I agreed to second Bill in his proposal to his Pigeon. In case the Pigeon didn't like his proposal, then I would pitch my own individual proposal.

"Do you have a budget?" Bill asked.

"How much money does the Pigeon have?" I asked.

He said, "I had our lawyer check it out and he's got maybe $500,000 to invest."

"Great. My budget is $500,000." He gets fifty percent of the film for five hundred thousand dollars . . . Five hundred thousand dollars will buy him fifty percent period."

Bill chuckled, shrugged his shoulders and shook his head.

"Well all right, Melvin," he said.

The more I thought about the figure, the better I liked it because it was simple, arithmetic-wise. Like I said, money acts. I'm okay with figures, but you should have the person you're trying to convince be able to follow you. Since money gets fifty percent of the action, and creativity accounts for the other half, I would in effect be offering 50 percent of the film for five hundred thousand dollars. I was sure that by leaving out most of my salary, I could bring in the film under that.

I had creamed spinach and Bill made his pitch. The businessman was young and nice looking which was reassuring. It meant he wouldn't be there for the potential bottoms he'd have to pinch. Bill and Steve talked long and convincingly but the businessman, despite his youth and looks, was only playing the game. Bill passed the ball to me.

"Perhaps you would be more interested in the way Melvin sees things." He wasn't.

Well I'm going to start shooting in the beginning of May," I announced grandly to everyone, including myself. "So you want in or you don't want in?"

"Are you sure about that date?" Bill asked me.

"Why that date," Steve said.

"I have to go on a publicity tour for *Watermelon Man* in

the middle of June . . . When I get asked about projects I don't want to talk about the film *I am going to shoot*, everybody does that, but about the *film I shot*.

As I said it, I realized that the thought must have been in my mind a long time. Anyway, it made perfect sense to me.

Talk about falling into place! Of course there was a little hitch of money. You know sometimes I think there is a Lord and he's a brother because he sure knows when to step in (sometimes).

"How are you going to finance?" the businessman said.

"Well I thought maybe you might come in for a bit . . ."

Silence.

" . . . Well I'll use my own money."

They all drew back as if I had planted a turd on the table.

"You must never use your own money," they chorused.

"You act as if the banks loan you money from the goodness of their hearts." I tried to reason with them. "Don't the banks charge you interest? . . . Why do you think they loan money? . . . You use your own money and the interest comes back to you."

"Well, I think by the use of my talents I'm putting in a big enough percentage, especially if I defer my salary," Bill said.

We weren't getting anywhere, the deaf talking to the deaf, as they say in France. Our positions were diametrically opposed. Fuck hedging a bet is the way I feel about it—if you believe in you, bet on you.

"If you had five hundred thousand dollars, would you invest it all in your film?" Bill asked me.

"Of course I would." And I meant it.

"I wouldn't," he said and he meant it. He shook his head and tried to laugh. "How are you going to distribute it when you finish?"

It must be terrible to be white, I thought.

"Nobody is doing anything—right. So there is going to be a product shortage."

"Your own money . . . but you don't have the five hundred thousand dollars, do you? How much do you think you can get?"

"Well I can come up with say, ninety to a hundred thousand, cash."

"How the hell can you do that? You were penniless last August."

"Well," I explained, "I still have about everything from *Watermelon Man*, the complete fifty thousand advance, plus most of the three hundred and fifty a week expense money plus bread from France and a couple of rich ladies who like me too."

"You would still be short about four hundred, Steve observed, "and money's tight."

"Money's very tight," the other two chorused. "How about your laboratory cost and your equipment? That takes a big chunk."

Remember I said Jesus was a brother? WHAMMO. Just then an idea struck me. The entire industry was hurting for money—right. Why didn't I go to the secondary source rather than the primary source? Instead of trying to raise money to pay the lab, why not go directly to the lab and make a deal . . . And that is what I did. Things began to fall in my favor. I went to Johnny Veitch, the head of production at Columbia, a film man from or to his fingertips and a no shit guy, and just told him frankly what I had on my mind and asked his advice about the lab.

He offered to call the labs personally and while I sat there. The first person he telephoned was Sid Solow, the President of a lab called C.F.I. I went to see him the next day and Mr. Solow gave me two pens, a felt pen and a ball point pen, and a little cardboard slide rule for converting feet into minutes, and a 100 percent deferral of all my lab expenses.

Security-wise, the laboratory deferral minimized another great danger—the danger of my negative accidentally getting scratched or something in the laboratory, which happens sometimes when you're working non-union or with controversial material. However since the lab wouldn't be paid until I finished the film, C.F.I, now, so to speak, was a partner with a vested interest, a financial stake to the tune of a hundred grand or so in my success.

Next I went to a big commercial bank in L.A. and said I wanted to open an account for my corporation. I was looking even more raggedy than usual and the bank manager treated me a little pompously, exactly as I had planned it.

"What's the name of your corporation?" he asked me.

"Yeah," I said.

He repeated the question.

"I heard you," I said. YEAH, INC., that's the name of my corporation.

His eyebrow went up a bit.

"It makes it easier to answer the phone," I said, putting on my shit-kicker act. I could just see the cat thinking what he had to go through some times. He didn't realize I was setting him up.

"My corporation is doing a film and I will be sending some money in to operate with."

Quaint! Yes, that's what he thought I was, quaint.

"I see, I see. When do you think this deposit will take place?"

"In the next few days," I said.

I went home took all the money I had and wired it to Bermuda or maybe it was the Bahamas, I don't remember, and then I had the money wired from there to the bank in Los Angeles. Then I got cleaned up and went back to the bank. It was a whole different ball game, after their receiving my seventy thousand dollars. Besides, I was enunciating like a mother fucker. The cat was bowled over. Couldn't figure out why he had had such a low opinion of me. He was very apologetic and he stayed apologetic which was right the fuck where I wanted him to be. So I set up my banking relationship.

The other expensive item was equipment. I went to Johnny Veitch and once again he came to the rescue, suggesting that since Columbia would defer me the equipment, I, in turn, would promise him first look at the film.

One other little nuisance developed called the completion bond. This is a guarantee that the film would not go over its cost, or if it did, the insurer of the completion bond would make up the difference. First to get a company to stoop to insure a film that didn't have a more classical production set up was impossiblesville and the premium alone if you did would kill you.

Well I came up with a fixed-budget idea. I said I would

bring in the film for half a million . . . I also said that I had some salary for myself built in . . . plus . . . I would have to give half a million plus creativity percentage, but notwithstanding, therefore by way of the completion bond, I wouldn't touch any of my salary if it would necessitate staying under the five hundred thousand mark. Already and Kilmanjaro is a mountain in Africa, yet the per capita rainfall in Iowa proved that . . . Actually, it was a whole lot of gobbledeegook, a little shaky at the seams maybe, but it seemed to work . . . Folks quit asking me about a completion bond.

Sure, the project had as many holes in it as swiss cheese and loose ends were dangling all over the place. Yet when I stood back and surveyed my baby, it looked pretty Goddamn good to me. Normally with luck, the script would have just passed up to the third flunky at some studio and here I was getting ready to go into gear.

It was nitty-gritty time and I went into what I call my pre-pre-production stage. I wanted a mobile, energetic and non-constipated crew to act as the backbone of the production. In Europe this type of crew is common but where was I to find such a team in America? Then I realized there were quite a few of these crews in operation. They weren't making the normal Hollywood fare, to be sure, but a whole parallel movie industry existed with everything from non-Union cameramen to non-Union theatrical house projectionists. Good old Puritanism! The unions had allowed the nudie makers to set up their own circuit rather than soil themselves with smut. Only in recent months have critics stooped to review these films even semi-seriously.

I discovered that there was a black man, Clyde Houston, working in nudies as a production manager, which was exactly what I needed. I called him and we arranged a meeting. I liked him from the first moment I saw him, and I thought I was a pretty good judge of character. He and I formed the pre-pre-production team. He knew Los Angeles like the back of his hand and set up schedules of locations for me to look at. Normally, pre-pre-production is fraught with tension but I thoroughly enjoyed every moment and slowly the setting took shape. It was almost as if I had each location in mind E.S.P. or something when I wrote the script. Everything seemed to be coming my way. All I lacked was the location of Beatle's brothel. WHAMMO. No sooner had I said that than the phone rang and an old lady of mine said that perhaps she had an idea for a place. Parents of an old boyfriend of hers lived in just that type of rambling black brick-a-brac-filled house. I rushed down and met some of the nicest people you could ever hope to meet, the Copeland family. Not only was the house perfect, but it was in a black section close to headquarters. Mr. Copeland worked in construction and was of invaluable service in several parts of the film. Mrs. Copeland prepared meals for the crew and practically the whole family acted in the film.

Clyde said he worked with a cameraman named Bob Maxwell who could do more with an ordinary flashlight than most photographers can do with a five-hundred-watt arc lamp. Bob turned out to be everything Clyde said he was and more. Not only was he a photographer (the head of lighting), he also worked as his own cameraman. I wanted two cameras going however, so I went to New

York and brought back José Garcia, recommended to me by Cliff Frasier who was in charge of the Community Film Workshop Council. I brought Tommy Scott in, a black that I had gotten to work on *Watermelon Man*, as José's assistant.

Bob Maxwell, besides being an excellent technician, had two other invaluable qualities—he was good-tempered and had endurance. He could hang in there hour after hour. If you aren't used to the tricks, long hours can play with your personality. This may not seem important, but I suspect it's one of the reasons parties are given at the completion of a film. From simple fatigue seven-eighths of the crew have grown to hate each other and a little celebration is needed to return everybody back to normal. Anyway, Bob could hang in there, and his crew could too. I suspect José also has this type of endurance, except he was recovering from a critical illness and was still weak, and we had to look out for him much to his annoyance.

White technicians should be chosen very carefully. More carefully perhaps than any other white person you deal with, if one operates at least the way I do, with the technician as an extension of myself. A creation at that point is usually in a formative stage and one may not be fully aware of oneself. So the vibes have to be even more than together. They have to be synonymous. The black usually has an advantage in dealing with the white, because way down deep in the old marrow of his bones, the whites don't look at him as an intellectual equal. If it's worked right, the situation can be milked with prodigious results. However, with the technician, you want to communicate with 100 percent efficiency, so he has to be ready not only to accept orders, but to accept the intellectual validity of your giving those orders.

I like to shoot with two cameras. The economy of this system is always touted, but for me its beauty lies in the type of editing it allows. If an actor does something I like in a scene and is not able to repeat it, I can always cut away to the other camera and then pick the same angle back up in another take. If I am shooting "Take 1" with cameras A and B and the actor does something I like, and then something I don't like, I simply have him pick up the action in "Take 2" again from the part I don't like or want. In the film editing, we can go from "Take 1, Camera A" to where I'm near the part I don't like, then switch to "Take 1 or Take 2 Camera B": and then a little later to "Take 1 or 2 Camera A". In other words, I'm covered at all times and working simply, extemporaneously and rapidly and aiming for naturalism from my actors. It was a perfect way to go.

I cast in the following way. I knew you couldn't keep anything a complete secret in Hollywood long, security or no security, and agents and agencies began to call. I explained I wasn't making a film for a major studio and wasn't interested in casting. This put the ball in their court. However, agents being agents, plus the film business being bad at the time, I was flooded with phone calls from morning to night.

The crew was all set: Bob and the basic shooting crew he normally worked with, including Nora, his wife, who took care of makeup, plus the additional people I had lined up, Clyde, Jose, Tommy, George, Priscilla, Diane and Tennyson. George: a writer-filmmaker with some helter-skelter film experience. Priscilla: sharp and sunny, energetic and thorough, with an extremely cute little turd cutter that she wagged provocatively. Good for morale. Priscilla had never been near a camera before, although she had been in films all of three months or so as an ordinary secretary. Diane: a college, student from Ohio, big kid, loyal, politically aware, spunky, but an erratic worker and always late, with no film experience. Tennyson: "Big T," a quick mind and a colossal body, again with no film experience . . .

At least everybody would always pitch in in anyway they could, I told myself.

I was now in the pre-production stage—nailing down locations and equipment, choosing the cast, laying out the polaroids I had taken of the people I had interviewed until I came to a satisfactory combination for a particular scene, overseeing costumes and props. I intended to rely very heavily on Clyde who had been indispensable during the pre-pre-production stage. However, his effectiveness seemed to decrease as we approached the zero hour. Of course, his being the most experienced in the camera crew, four times the amount of work fell on his shoulders and I thought it was just a phase. George, who was acting as his second, probably because George had less experience, was very resourceful and seemed to grow as Clyde became more ineffectual. George's thin film experience wasn't enough to hang him up on my unorthodox approach.

I surveyed the scene and tried to look toward the weeks ahead the best I could. I put Diane on props, and wardrobe under Priscilla, who was production secretary. Tennyson was my Friday. George was second assistant, assistant set decorator and Clyde's assistant. Clyde was production manager and first assistant. I was producer, director, deco-rator and in charge of casting plus, as it later turned out, script supervisor and lead. I had made several demoral-izing tries to find a star for *Sweetback*. The trouble was that the actors who had enough technique were too much in some form of the Man's bag, and those who would have been spiritually right didn't have enough technique (not acting technique but cinematic know-how to work at the pace we would be going), or the temperament. I find some blows harder to take than others, I suppose everybody does, and not finding the lead troubled me immensely. I think what I felt was despair and since that was one God-damn thing I couldn't afford, I did it myself.

So time went on. I suppose I should have been a little concerned about my load, but concern is a funky luxury when a lot has to be done. Anyhow, it beats the post office, I told myself.

Besides, there were other pressing little details. I was still short of some of the minimum bread. But there are always blessings. My agent had left me, shaking his head in triplicate at my self-destructive course, my lack of mod-esty and the pornographic script of which he had read only three paragraphs. (One of the security measures I had adopted was telling everyone I was making a nudie film.) I was calling everyone or thing I could think of, looking for money. Once I thought I was close to twenty thousand dollars when I was put on to a black brother in medicine. He made an appointment to see me that very evening. He came looking very dapper in a jump suit and he brought a good-looking young couple with him, maybe it was a menage à trois. We talked half the night and he said he would let me know the next day. Three days later I hadn't heard from him, so I knew the deal was dead, but because of the hope that springs eternal in the human breast, etc., I got a call through to him. He was having financial setbacks at the moment, etc., etc. However, one night the pretty little girl appeared at my door and gave me some pussy, so all wasn't lost.

I had done one of Bill Cosby's television series so I called him.

"Bill," I said, "I'm making a film and I need some bread."

"How much do you need?" Bill said.

"Well, it's going to cost five hundred thousand."

"That's not what I asked you," Bill said in his pleasant, kind voice.

"Fifty thousand, I need fifty thousand more."

"You got it," Bill said.

I was speechless, overcome by relief and pride. Well, all I had to do now was get ready to start. And here comes that old pot-gutted, snaggle-toothed broad called Disaster.

She came in the disguise of a phone call from the Screen Actors Guild. Priscilla took the call. She turned toward me with her hand over the receiver with a worried look on her face.

"What is it," I asked.

"A man from the Screen Actors Guild has called several times but you weren't here and I didn't have the chance to tell you."

"So?"

"Well he said he must talk to you immediately."

As it so happened, all the YEAH people were there

going over the last minute preparations. Long ago, someone, it had to be George or Clyde, remarked that we might run into difficulty with SAG if we used Union people. But after a while, I guess I sort of dropped that fear. The room got so quiet you could have heard a rat pissing on cotton. (Headquarters during the entire shooting was—my kitchenette, a composite living room, office, kitchen and bedroom.) I took the call in the bedroom. The man from SAG said very politely that I had forgotten to register the production with their office, but he knew it was just an oversight in the chaos of production. I went to numbersville.

Just what did the oversight consist of. Yeah . . . oversight . . . yeah, oversight . . . However, he said if I had not recti-fied the oversight by the following day, they would be forced to put up a notice forbidding any of their people to work on the film. Well, I asked him what did my oversight run, and he started reading off numbers of lines, special insurance, posting bond, etc. Anyway, it was going to cost bread, a lot of bread. At that moment, if they were going to sell Los Angeles for a nickel, I would have had to run to keep from being sold with it. I was sleeping on the couch, I didn't have money to pay for a room for Diane, etc. (This eventually worked out because one of the other out of town crew members who had a salary plus room and board, started shacking up with a young lady he ran into, so I moved Diane into his place.)

Well, there was nothing I could do, so I went to indig-nationsville and told the cat to shove the whole thing up his third cousin's ass. I raised my voice in firm authority, slammed down the phone, took a deep breath and came out of the bedroom. You've heard of a pregnant pause? Silence, dead silence and all eyes on me.

"Well, we can't use any SAG people," I announced.

"What are we going to do?"

"Re-cast," I said. "Re-cast," I repeated with more conviction. I suppose I would have felt something, except my act was so good I was beginning to go along with my own bullshit, chug-chugging on my cigar.

"I'll call Bob Maxwell right now." Clyde said.

"Bob? What for?" I said.

"Well, we're going to have to postpone a week, right?"

We were five days from the start. NO! May 11th it was and May 11th it would be. I don't mean to be Pollyannaish, but maybe that extra crisis helped us because the tension that had been mounting had an outlet. Anyway, here's my hand to heaven, the Lord be my judge, yeh, though I walk through the valley . . . we were going to make it.

The countdown started but not before the first crack appeared in the whole solidarity of the YEAH personnel. Priscilla had asked for a part in the film and with her school-girlish face and figure, I thought she would be perfect as the ingenue, seduced by the lesbian-qua-Sweetback in the brothel show. I had chosen that scene for my very first day of shooting. I made the choice for two reasons— one because it was sexy and securitywise it would throw snoopers off the trail. And two because it was one of the most involved scenes of choreography, requiring the largest number of people per space and it would be good to get it out of the way.

The day before we were to begin, Priscilla came to me to tell me she wasn't going to do it, she had changed her mind. I tried to persuade her, but it seemed her main boyfriend didn't want her to do it.

"But you told me you had asked him already."

"I did but . . .

"But what?"

"Well, I hadn't explained it to him really."

She offered to leave the film, I could have broken her legs, and I told her the next time, I would.

"Anyhow, it wasn't important," she said.

She never had set foot on a production before, and there she was, making directorial decisions. Well, ain't nothing new. Like they say, mother-fucking familiarity breeds mother-fucking contempt. I called another woman I was going to use in another scene and she agreed to do the part.

So I had to sacrifice a real actress because there was no one who looked the part, and it was going to have to be a role of composition. So I would read the script every day like a carpenter, stroking the wood, studying the grain. That's how I came up with the glob method. It always had seemed to me that 80 percent or so of the criss-crossing, back and forth from location to location to location that went on in a film, was bullshit: we will start here in the morning, J. B., then go over there at noon, then come back here for pickups afterwards, and everybody nods and runs off in fifteen different directions.

Something or somebody always has to be accommodated, anything from a star's toilet whims to lighting to the weather, you name it. Maybe roaming over to some

NEW place was the final goal, some tinkling sense of accomplishment that we were all searching for. Yeah, maybe that's it. Anyway, T.M.A.L.S.S., that tinkling sense (if that's what it was) was just too rich for my blood.

Time lost and gas lost, as big a pain as that was, were chicken feed compared to the man-power and brain-power lost in the logistics of moving everybody from location to location and back to location. Probably half of what the layman thinks is going on in a film can be traced back to this jumping around. This was especially important because I was planning to economize by not hiring a script supervisor or at least I thought I was. But at the last minute, my production manager, second assistant, and assistant editor persuaded me I couldn't live without one. The very first day of shooting, I had just gotten up off the actress and was placing my camera for the next set-up, when, I remember it like it was yesterday, the script supervisor saunters up. Anyway, it seemed like he was sauntering, and it was one of THOSE scenes so I was in my birthday suit to boot.

"You won't be able to edit this without a triple-domojajo-reversal-pan so you must reshoot," the script man said.

I fired the sonofabitch on the spot. Frankly, I didn't know what a triple reversal, or whatever it was called, was and as for it being so essential to my editing, I already had figured out how I was going to cut the scene and no God-damn body was going to start telling me how . . . Besides he thought he was too good to help the rest of us load equipment that morning, etc., etc. . . . . Actually, I didn't fire him . . . I turned him into an extra.

I divided my shooting into chunks that used the same

people in the same costumes and called it a glob. For example, a typical glob in conception and execution was the motorcycle encounter and fuck-out with Big Sadie. Normally it would have been shot over a period of several days with probably other scenes mixed in. I hired a motorcycle gang and locked the doors. I couldn't find an abandoned warehouse with the right wiring and price, so I hired a theater that was empty for the moment. I used the stage, which allowed me low angles for shooting. Very effective composition with the ramp and wood I built on the stage. I just dug the idea of a ramp. Under the glob method, no one was allowed to leave until his shooting was completely finished. Voilà, in one swoop, no absentee-extra problems, a plague to second assistants, and no costume-changing problems. No continuity problems for the script boy, which was me again, having demoted the second script boy down to an extra.

A couple of big globs ran into fifteen or sixteen hours of continuous shooting, but what with the high esprit of the crew which was infectious, the size of "Big T," and a couple of other "friends" brought in on special occasions, plus no one getting paid until the glob was over, there was never an overshoot or a recall. (Well, except for once when a generator we had tied to the back of a car slipped and went crashing onto the asphalt.)

Crude, but it did it, and after all the dust has settled . . . That's where it's at—ghetto-wise, anyway.

The plan for shooting followed the simplicity of necessity, of life itself. Anyway, life on those rare occasions when the bullshit is gone.

Uncle Abner was the most successful small-time crook

and contented man I ever knew. He never got busted because everyone knew, even the cops, that there was no evidence. He carried it all in his head. One summer day he sent me to get him a Royal Crown Cola. When I came back, he asked me what I wanted.

"A nickel tip," he held out the nickel in front of me, "or a million dollar tip?" He tapped the side of his head.

I could have bought an ice cream bar with the nickel, but the bigger boys would have taken it away from me anyway, so what did I have to lose.

"The million dollar tip," I said.

Uncle Abner was very pleased. "Folks wonder how I do it . . . I looks for the logic and then jest keep it simple . . . as simple as you can."

I thought it was high time to cash in on Uncle Abner's tip. Anyway, the shooting was to go in order of flexibility, starting with the least flexible cornerstone pieces at the beginning and finishing up with alternate scenes and any new ideas that might develop.

I told a lie. At the beginning, I swore that I wasn't going to use 16 mm, that I was going to make a big film, that I was going to shoot entirely in 35 mm. I over-used the rule of thumb about 35 mm being big, professional, etc., and 16 mm equaling amateursville, low-budget. Both production value and professional quality are determined more by what's going on in front of the lens and how it is recorded than by what film stock is in the camera magazine. We decided to use 16 mm in the streets for four reasons: its two usual advantages, economy of the stock and the mobility of 16 mm equipment; third, security reasons: 16 mm is less noticeable, minimizing police hassles and

16 mm is also taken less seriously by Hollywood types, minimizing union hassles. My last reason for using 16 mm was for its texture—a paradox, because texture is exactly what is considered the big drawback of 16 over 35. 16 mm is more grainy, less slick than 35 mm, i.e., more newsreely, more documentary. The more I thought about it, the more I felt 16 would even add to the flavor of realism I wanted in the street.

Shit-though-all-in-all, I figured, theoretically and planning-wise, I wasn't doing bad. Outside of switching to 16 mm, the big picture was pretty much as I had up-front planned it, program-wise. There were people running around and equipment being shuffled . . . (Maybe the thing really was going to come into existence . . . But the story about the guy who thought he could fly and jumped off the ledge of a tenth story building was always yapping at the heels of my mind. As he went past the third story window, someone stuck out his head and asked him how he was doing. He replied, O.K. so far . . .

. . .

FIRST DAY OF SHOOTING
BATTLE CRY TO MYSELF

Let's do the mother fucker. Existence is the game. Existence is ten-tenths of the game. Maybe possession is nine-tenths, but if it don't exist, you can't possess it, right. If you fathered the image of your concept of the universe you already got them fighting on your territory, right. Let's make the motherfucker and see what happens.

. . .

FIRST DAY: MAY 11TH
COPELAND'S GLOBL.
FREAK SHOW.
WE LOST OUR CHERRY IN STYLE.

CAUTION UNRESOLVED: Bob semi-complains. He is not used to working under such tight supervision. Delicate moment when the girl undressed and the lesbian wearing the dildo undressed and got down to the nitty gritty. The crowd of extras playing onlookers were on the verge of freaking right out of character. The buszwazee getting ready to be offended and the street folks getting ready to hop down on the floor and get to it too. I played my trump security-margin-card.

"DAD, would you move your chair over there just a bit."

(DAD?! HIS FATHER'S HERE! HE WOULD LET HIS OWN FATHER COME HERE!)

"Over a little to the left, DAD."

My father moved his chair to the left.

(IF HIS FATHER'S HERE, THINGS REALLY MUST BE ON THE UP AND UP.)

"No DAD that's a little too much. Over to the right some. A little more . . ."

My dad moved his chair back bit by bit. I sneaked a couple of glances out of the corner of my eye. A sense of the occasion seemed to have been restored. And by this time, my father's chair was about back in its original place.

"Thanks, DAD," I said. My dad smiled his warm, dignified smile. I wondered if he knew.

Bob's crew is extraordinary . . . YEAH people really pitching in . . . We got a big one out of the way . . .

● ● ●

SECOND DAY: MAY 12TH
GLOB 2-GLOB 5.
RAIDING PARTY.
BEATLE WITH HIS PETS.

Yesterday's caution resolved, Bob loved the rushes. During lunch break we saw the first day of rushes. *Spies from the Unions were in the projection booth, hunch was right.* I screened the juiciest parts first. By the second reel, all the Union spies and everyone else in the projection, booth believed I was making a fly-by-night nudie like I said I was. Bob said he really loved what he saw and we shook hands.

(Day glided by so well, I just knew trouble was lurking.)

THIRD DAY: MAY 13TH
BEATLE'S INTERROGATION——GLOB 3.
BATHROOM——GLOB 4.
POOLHALL FIGHT——GLOB 6.

YEAH people begin to actually show the signs of the strain. Everybody complains about the first assistant . . . Second assistant wants to leave . . . my housemother duties begin. Move Diane to her own place . . . *Ordered everybody to bed early.*

● ● ●

The teamwork smoothed out and the days blurred into each other. A few notes and sometimes an incident like a twig on a frozen lake would melt through the fatigue, an escape from the relentless current of activity, and settle lightly to the bottom on the memory of my mind . . .

The lamps overloading the wiring in the motel sequences . . . Shooting the whole thing with reflectors, two catching the sun and relaying the light to two more, . . . Fighting with my main girl and falling out—not speaking because she didn't want me to use my own son in the title sequence where Sweetback loses his cherry . . . The time when the actor heard there might be trouble and showed up carrying a gun, a loaded .38. I made him leave it behind, but a couple of nights later when he showed up for his gun, I couldn't find it. I looked everywhere. I questioned the folks the next day when they reported to work. Everyone said Diane had it and when she came in I lit into her about taking the gun out of the room.

"It's here," she countered . . . I said, "It couldn't be." I had looked everywhere . . . "No it's here . . ."

"Where did you put it?" . . . "With the guns in the prop box." Sometimes, I suppose when I get the time, I'll have a recurring nightmare about that escape. The actors playing cops and detectives must have been in and out of that prop box at least fifty times or more to get their guns all .38 police specials just like the loaded one.

SHIT SERIOUS AS A HEART ATTACK

Bread so low we can't pick up a new shipment of film stock. . . . Two days before Payroll . . . In short, the corporation was down to thirteen dollars when Cosby cosigned for fifty grand, thirteen dollars and I am not even superstitious . . .

The night I got the bread, a girl friend came over and brought me some dinner she had fixed for me. My ass was dragging, dragging, but I had such a serene feeling . . . I wondered how come, then I remembered the new bread in the bank. The girl had made collards. She had eaten already but she sat at the table anyway. I guess because I was so tired or something, I let it all hang out. Talking to her about the goals I had set for the film, and not wanting to let the brothers and sisters down. The sister was so sympathetic, it was good to rap to her. I talked on about how worried I had been about the bread and how if I had had to shut down operations, what it would have done to the morale, what a narrow escape it had been. . . . Oh, I was never worried, she said. Goddamn, I felt like a king when she said that. The sister had that much confidence in me.

"You had that much confidence in me?" I fished. (I should have left well enough alone.)

"Not exactly," she explained . . . Confidence in me had nothing to do with it . . . It seemed I was a Leo with his asshole rising to the something that month or some shit like that plus my seventh house converging . . .

"Fuck you," I said. "Your seventh house is converging on my shit house."

She blew her top and told me that's why niggers weren't nowhere because they didn't pay attention to the ancient wisdom of the stars . . . I was running low on old ladies but I never could bring myself to apologize to her because, Goddamn, I didn't feel like apologizing. Anyway, the film role being what it was, I was pussy-whipped as it was.

• • •

THE SEVENTH DAY OF SHOOTING: 6:15 A.M.

I had an actress crisis. Then I remembered a girl who I thought had eyes for me so I called her, she answered all sleepy-voiced, "who is it?"

"Melvin. You remember, you were up to my office one day." (I don't pull the office bit shit, but this was an emergency.)

"Oh, Melvin," her voice picked up.

"Is you gonna give me some pussy or not?" I said, laying it right out.

"Hee, hee, " she grinned.

If you grin, you in, as they say on the block.

"I would like to go out with you sometime, " she said. (Talk about euphemism. Now comes the delicate part.)

"Look, there will be a few people on our . . . ah . . . ah . . . date." Now she had to be thinking did I know something she didn't know I knew, which I didn't . . ."just watching."

6:25: Crisis over, she agreed. She was reporting for her *date* at 8:30 and everything was cool until the part where she had to be nude. To put her at ease, I got into my birthday suit first. Then she got into hers. We started to embrace passionately when my kids, whom I had forgotten were arriving from S.F., appeared.

"Hi, Dad," they said.

Luckily, kids are always hungry, so I had one of the crew take them to eat. I told him to get my son a hamburger . . . He was a hamburger freak at the time. And I told him to get my daughter a BLT . . . She was a BLT freak at the time.

The eighth day when I was shooting the funeral, a junkie kept bugging us about whether he could lie in the coffin . . . Once he came and started banging at the door, needle in hand, asking me for help to get the vein . . . And when my son's big day came and the actress put her legs around him, he looked so much like someone going down for the third time that everybody cracked up so hard we had to take a break . . . George quit,—heat of the

oven. . . . The car exploding just as we were losing light . . .
I have the CLAP.

MAY 28TH: THE 13TH DAY OF SHOOTING

That thirteen again and like I said I'm not even superstitious. I had split up the crew into two units and the second
unit was missing. I was doing Sweetback shoots on the outskirts of town for inter-cutting, and José was shooting some
inner-city second unit footage. They were an hour overdue,
then two hours, then four hours. At ten o'clock that night
José called. They were in jail. They had not even been
filming when the cops got them. They were driving down
the street when the police pulled them over. The cops came
to the paneled truck with their guns drawn and ordered
everybody out of the vehicle. They said they thought Josh's
telephoto lens was a bazooka. But when they discovered
their mistake, they didn't let them go. (The crew consisted
of José, who is very light-skinned but speaks with a Puerto
Rican accent, Tommy and Tennyson who are both black,
and Dennis who might have been acceptable except he had
a hippie beard and hairdo.) They conducted an illegal
search of the truck and found a magazine with a feature
article on community organization . . . So even though their
papers were in order, they booked them on grand theft and
impounded all the equipment including the paneled truck.
They handcuffed everyone and began to hassle them about
being militants. They were picked up at five on their way
back to the office, but no one was allowed to make a call
until after 9:30 P.M. After 9:00 P.M., all the judges who could
give a writ for immediate release are unreachable.

I talked to José on the phone and he explained the

situation. They wanted me to come down and get them out. I told them I couldn't. At least come try and visit. I couldn't. It was too dangerous. Melvin Van Peebles, the director of a major motion picture from a major studio, was a tall, slightly aristocratic white man who wore a double-breasted suit and would have much more power to get them released than the raggedy, wild-looking brother I was. And suppose the cops just decided to keep me too. José saw where I was coming from. It was very rough on him because he was required to take pills for his illness but we were not allowed to get them in to him after he ran out. I asked what the tariff was, and he told me everybody had been booked the maximum twelve hundred and fifty dollars bail each.

I got on it immediately, working the double-breasted aristocrat angle. Two days and a thousand dollars in cash later (10 percent of the total five thousand dollars bail to the bondsman and five hundred to the lawyer) everybody was sprung. At last I felt it was safe enough to show my face and go down to pick up the truck. The cops charged me twenty-nine dollars more, for towing and storing my truck which they had taken away from my crew, even though the charges were dropped. One of the brothers who had been down there for a long time felt I had let him down, and was talking about ripping me off. I couldn't lay low until his depression passed, and I couldn't compromise the film by defusing him, so I just continued on . . . sticking in the shadows whenever I was out at night to avoid being too tempting a target, and other shit like that that I had learned in the movies.

Man, when shit don't go right, it just don't go right.

One evening after almost everyone had left, one of the girls on the crew was still sitting and looking . . . (stare-stare) Man, was she looking.

"Ain't no use in looking at me like that," I told her. My ass was dragging so bad between worrying about bullets and bills and with the whipping that the penicillin had laid on my ass, you couldn't have melted me and poured me on a girl. But the seat the poor girl was sitting on was practically smoking she was so horny. Then I got an inspiration. One of the crew had fallen asleep in the corner. I shook him awake and told him I thought he was too tired to drive home. Then I asked the girl, since she lived so close by, if she would take him home with her. Her smile lit up the room, as they say. But the next morning she came in with her jaws clenched tight and her bottom lip looking real unbangified. The cat only swung one way . . . the other way, and I hadn't picked up on it.

Strained. My people were strained to the breaking point so I gave them time off.

• • •

JUNE 2ND: EVENING.
EVERYBODY HAS PERFORMED ABOVE AND BEYOND THE CALL OF DUTY.
BUT THEY'VE HAD IT.
Bob and I will have to take it from here.

• • •

JUNE 3RD: 18TH DAY OF SHOOTING.
Bob, Kenny (his assistant), Nora, Diana, and me go to the desert. *Luck came our way. Great day.*

• • •

JUNE 4TH: THE LAST DAY OF SHOOTING.

IT HAS TAKEN NINETEEN DAYS OF SHOOTING.
(Twenty, counting the day the second unit went to test the film emulsion.)
THE MOTHER FUCKER IS OVER!

• • •

JUNE 5TH.

We have a party and realize how fond we've grown of one another. We begin to see the fucking immensity of what we've done.

• • •

JUNE 6TH: 6:00 A.M.

I began to edit the film.

• • •

I think it was Eisenstein who said that a film can be made or broken in the editing room. This is true, but a film can be broken, perhaps not made, but surely broken at almost any stage of the filmmaking process. Since my original up-front programming only carried me through the completion of the shooting specifically, I appended another up-front program to my plan for the post-production. Mostly, it was pretty general guide-lining because the variables, since I had no time to edit during the shooting, were endless.

UP-FRONT EDITING PROGRAM

1. Don't understand the film too quickly. Sure, it was my baby, but I must not be too possessive.

Be a good parent to the child. The film had a life of its own now, it was in there somewhere, my job was to find that life and nurture, it. This is what editing is all about. At least as I see it. Anyway, T.M.A.L.S.S., like they say on the block, if it don't fit, don't force it.

2. I'm lazy and I was tired. So rather than leave it to my own initiative, I set up a work schedule: six in the morning to eight at night, Monday through Friday, eight to six on Satur- days; nine to four on Sundays.

I also made a promise to myself to be very strict about showing any of the editing to people as I went along. Wisely, knowing my weakness, I didn't incorporate it in my up-front program, I just wasn't able to muster up that much self-control. Jesus, suddenly I would begin to get something together after staring at the image on the Moviola screen for hours. My impulse always was to show it to someone. No, I would tell myself. The scene isn't pol- ished and they won't know how it fits into the whole (usu- ally I didn't even know how it was going to fit into the whole). In the meantime, while I was going through all of these gyrations, my feet would be heading for the door to find somebody to buttonhole. It never failed though, I was right in the first place. No one ever saw how the scene was going, let alone where it was going, but the next time a cut jelled, there would be, out in the corridor again looking for my spectator . . . Frankly, I love editing. At last you have the material in your hand. The canvas has been prepared, the paints mixed and there you are. Minus of course, depending on the way the scene is shot, details such as finished sound, music, etc. But these things a professional accounts for almost automatically.

Solitude, just you and the film and the equipment. Your assistants are essentially an extension of the equipment, freeing you from the highly complex mechanical chores, sort of a living liaison from one piece of equipment to the other.

Living, aye, and that's the rub of it. There's something very vulnerable about a certain moment in creativity. Freud defined creating as opening the floodgates of the mind and letting all possibilities and impossibilities rush in—the wild, the rational, the irrational, the fantastic—then sifting the sluice. Sort of like witch-doctors used to do when they would throw the bones to make a prophecy. I think that moment when the floodgates are thrown open is that super-vulnerable point in creating. Your general state should be as neutral as possible; any impurity takes on immense proportion. My first week of editing was exhilarating, but there was something else there, something I couldn't catch. Finally I realized what it was. I was miserable.

My assistant didn't approve of me. If I had had a number of assistants as a feature film normally would have had, maybe things would have balanced out a little, but breadwise, it wasn't possible. I had only hustled enough money to carry me through the completion of the shooting. Breadwise, I was hurting, hurting, hurting. My assistant's presence represented humanity, all of humanity. It's a tiring mother fucker—trying to open the floodgates of your mind with a sack of humanity's disapproval on your back.

Sack of humanity's disapproval or not, my assistant, work-wise, carried his load. My beacon, my balm, was a French expression about hunching your shoulders and getting on with it. But I have to admit, I was heart-broken, I had so looked forward to the editing phase. Then in my darkest hour, here comes that most beautiful and radiant of all damsels, lady good luck. No, I'm not ashamed to talk about luck, it does exist, it's just that since people have no control over it they fear it, also you can be seduced by it, but never forget the mother fucker can turn on you in a second, kissing your ass one minute and knocking your head off the next. When it's GOOD, ride it for all it's worth, when it's BAD, stick in the clinch so it can't get a clean swing at you. Anyway, to make a long story short, the assistant didn't have the same amount of scruples contract-wise, and one day he announced to me that he was leaving. I even put on a long face for the form of the thing.

The assistant said he had the ideal replacement and brought me a kid named Jerry who had never even worked in 35 mm before, but was bright and enthusiastic. Plus he had stamina and he was hungry so I gave him a trial. At the beginning, his attention level was much too low, geared to an amateurish type of filmmaking. But that shit got straightened out fast and he learned to really hang in there. He matched my hours and I agreed to take him on. Mouthwise, the kid had to be cooled off every now and then. He tended to over-simplify, his main drag was that he was unaware of what he was ignorant of—I guess that's the definition of being ignorant in the first place, anyhow, ain't it.

I was happy. Sure there were creative anxieties and

editing problems and money hassles and everybody laughing behind my back and the doom-sayers doing their number. When I first started it was HE'LL NEVER GET IT OFF THE GROUND. Then when I was in pre-production, HE'LL NEVER RAISE THE MONEY. Then when I was shooting, HE'LL NEVER FINISH IT, HE'LL RUN OUT OF MONEY BEFORE THE SHOOTING IS OVER. Then when editing began, HE WON'T BE ABLE TO PUT IT TOGETHER AND HE'LL NEVER BE ABLE TO SELL IT. Shit, I didn't mind that. Jesus Christ was nothing but a carpenter in his own home town—right. I knew what I had from the first mother-fucking day of rushes, from the first mother-fucking day I zipped my fly back up. What bugged me was I couldn't tell them, I was still too vulnerable, security-wise. I had to still keep it low keyed.

I was doing the old tight-rope number. Shit, I was born and bred on a tight rope, but I let it look like I was in immediate, imminent, momentary danger of falling. That way, since I was surely going to break my ass on my own, no one, supposing someone were so inclined, would feel they would have to bother to cut the rope. Sometimes life is a bitch. I had some good friends on the lot, especially among the technicians, some great guys who went up against the wall to help, especially in wardrobe and sound and transportation. It's a bitch, isn't it, that the way life's drawn up, your time is spent in plotting against enemies instead of rejoicing in friends.

Yep, to tell it like it is, I was happy. Sometimes, I would even hum that song about doing it my way . . . meaning, I would get out of bed or off the couch, brush my teeth and get dressed if I wasn't. Some nights I would just come home and lay on the couch with my clothes on; sometimes I would call Anna who looked at life through the same lenses as I did and touch base with the world outside. Anyway, I would go down the steps, turn left and start down the sidewalk. Straight in front of me on the far side of Sunset a couple of miles away, Hollywood had been written on a mountain, and when it wasn't too foggy, I could make out the dull gray letters by the dawn's early light. Half-way towards Sunset, I turned left and ducked under the chain and took a short cut through the parking lot. Another left and I would be at the guard's gate of Columbia Studios where I was editing the film.

When the coffee truck arrived about a quarter to seven, the guard would call my extension and let me know and I would walk down and get my coffee. By the time I carried my cup back to the editing room, the sun would be getting its first good peek, sometimes the only peek for the day, through the smog. My windows faced the East and I would open up the Venetian blinds for a moment while I contemplated the universe, the sun and my coffee. Sun and coffee are dynamite at five minutes to seven. Like I said, I was happy. Jerry and I would work through until ten minutes to eight or so. Then we'd go up to Brewer's, the greasy spoon around the corner on Sunset. It closed at eight and sometimes we would have a race. I could run faster, but Jerry could jump the guard barriers, and we always ended up in a tie. I'd have short ribs of beef and he'd have roast beef dinner with lots of gravy on his potatoes.

Talk about solitude. Who takes a maverick nigger with a hippie assistant seriously? We were so low on the totem pole that unless I had a moment of weakness and buttonholed somebody to look at a cut or something, we weren't even bothered with kibitzers.

I hadn't been able to deal with film so purely for thirteen years (there's that number again) when I had to sell my car to make my first short movie. My problems were purely creative problems, at least the ones I was dealing with. (Bread was the big scare. Even Cosby's attorneys had started in on my ass about money. But Rick Johnson, a young black lawyer with whom I had formed a pact, was keeping all the wolves at the door cooled out. The deal was he would watch my back legal-wise, and I would teach him all I knew mogul-wise.) It was almost as if I were writing a book.

Of course, ivory tower honesty can get you into a lot of trouble. At least it got me into a lot of trouble thirteen years ago. I remember it as well as yesterday. I had set up my little 16 mm editing board in the closet, the only dark place in our apartment. I was working three jobs, I had taken in a boarder and I was taking care of the kids while my wife at the time went to school. One day, she slunk her head into the closet. I was right in the middle of my purity.

"What would you say," she said, "if I told you I was sleeping with the roomer?"

Like I said, I was deep in my purity, so I told the truth.

"I'd raise his rent, I said.

You know I think that was the beginning of the end, marriage-wise. Notwithstanding, I dig purity—no one to please, or to try to understand but my MUSE . . . I was happy.

I edited the film with the same logic I went in shooting it; i.e. the cornerstone non-flexible pieces I edited first. I remember the first scene I edited was Beatle's bathroom soliloquy. I edit with three or four picture heads at once. I think this practice will become very prevalent in the future, but for now it's still pretty much of an oddity. To me, old-time editors seem to spend half their time comparing pieces of film. Is this shot better than another shot? They take it out of the Moviola, look, put in the new shot, take that out, put in the other shot. To me it seems much simpler to look at both shots at the same time. Hence, I had a Moviola constructed with three screen "heads" for viewing so I could look at three different shots at the same time and compare more easily.

I had another normal Moviola with a single screen head for any wild freeshots I might have taken. This is where my use of two cameras really came in handy. For example, I would usually decide rather easily that one "A" shot I had taken was better than the other, so I would put it up as one of the images on the three-headed Moviola. Then I would also put up the two "B" shots—the one shot simultaneously with the "A" I had kept, and the one from the "A" I had, discarded. Then any inter-cutting shooting that I might want to get fancy with I would put up on my normal single screen Moviola.

Now I could look at all four images and begin to get an idea of where I was at with the least amount of film juggling.

Finally, there was old Beatle on all four screens standing there doing his thing. Which angle did I want on him while he was saying "brother"—the front or the side? In which take does he sit on the toilet more naturally, one or two? Two. Okay. But from which angle on take two—"A" or "B"? Where

115

do I want to change angles? Do I want to cut there and shorten the dialogue? Searching for the right combinations looking for the code, the key, digging for the essence . . .

Finally the scene was finished, and it felt right—NO, felt my ass, I KNEW it was right. Of course, the scene would be tightened another one or more times before the editing was finally finished, but there was my rough outline and I went along with it and dug it all the way.

One of the worst things about filmmaking is that you're limited to the level of intelligence of the guy you're trying to get bread from. This is especially true and frustrating if you're doing anything really innovative. When MONEY can't understand, you're usually in trouble, breadwise; in the first place if he could understand it as a projection forward into a new universe, he would be the artist. For example, take the breaking of Beatle's eardrums. I don't feel I would have been able to do these opticals for a major company because they wouldn't have understood the final visual end at the beginning and so wouldn't have laid out the money.

Suppose a painting cost as much as a film. Imagine Cezanne trying to get someone to give him a million dollars to make a painting. He wouldn't have been able to get off the ground. Of course Delacroix would have. Delacroix would go to the patron and say, "Look, I want to do this painting. There's going to be this woman half-drowning on a raft, you'll see a titty too, and then right around the raft you're going to see a shark, and a storm might be coming up and maybe there'll be a boat way in the background representing hope."

"I can see it, I can see it," the patron would yell, "You've got the bread."

And Cezanne comes in and says, "I want to do an orange." The cat says, "An orange? Where's the plot? And besides, people have already done oranges. What's the matter with you kid, are you some kind of egomaniac or something? You think you're better than Monet or Chardin or something?"

And he would name the whole list of all the people who had done oranges . . ."And besides, still lifes aren't selling so hot right now."

"It's different, Sir." Anyone might try to explain.

"How different can an orange be, already, for Christ sake . . . after all, an orange is an orange . . . What kind of freak are you anyway? I've got this aunt living in the out-house and she always says etc. . . .

But a Cezanne orange isn't like any other orange. And it only makes sense in the image itself, in the visual, the actual visual. It's not literature, it's painting. Some of the heaviest cats who have ever been in cinema defy description in purely verbal story line terms. Just as an orange only gives us the vaguest inkling of a Cezanne orange until we see it, verbal descriptions of Charlie Chaplin's *City Lights* or Kurosawa's *MacBeth* don't begin to touch the cinematic dimensions of the films themselves, no more than a concert can encompass a novel by Richard Wright.

But words are cheap, like they say, and film's expensive. So we continue to try to make one medium do the work of another. The cinematic qualities in American films are usually by-products because an American film is usually literature first. Sometimes you can almost hear the patron yelling, "I can see it, I can see it." Sometimes I would be plotting the freezes and changes and color combinations in an optical sequence and I would begin to smile to myself. I could just imagine me trying to explain to some guy who doesn't understand film in the first place the freeze frame or the color change, etc., etc., inherent in, say, just the motorcycle opticals . . . Like impossiblesville. I can hear the guy saying, "Well, I've got this aunt living in Topeka and she always says," etc.

Eighty percent of the creative energy that I put into *Watermelon Man* went into the corridors of power wrestling for the freedom to direct the film as I saw fit. In Europe, the director is sort of like the captain of the ship. In America, he's just a member of a committee, and not even the chairman at that.

My right eye had gone out on me from overwork, and I was wearing a patch over it. There I was, Walter Mitty-time, a pirate captain calmly pouring over the charts in his cabin while the storm raged outside: technical waves (I had to use two different sets of optical people to get the results I wanted, one brilliant but spaced out, the other expert but numb) and financial gale winds (people started wanting their bread back so bad until I thought it best to start walking in the old shadows again.)

But I had a good crew, Jerry and Brother Rick. We were a little short-handed but we were doing it and ghetto-wise or anywhere else doing it is where it's at. The secretary had asked leave to abandon ship, pleading a weak stomach. Her request had been granted forthwith but we sailed on, never wavering in our course, with me pouring over the charts, actually my Moviolas, looking for gold, actually the essence, the key, the code to the scenes.

Each time I came to a new section, I would gather all the material and run it until I almost knew it by heart. But then I wouldn't simply begin to boil it down by the numbers. I would sit down in the cracked old saggy sack that used to be a stuffed chair, with a towel over my face, or squat on one of the concrete logs by the row of buildings across the way, and I'd study my boot tips in the gravel or sit on the throne in the editing room toilet and leaf through *The Pictorial History of Crime* or stretch out on the editing room floor with the towel over my head. It looked like I was goofing off but I would be trying to open my floodgates and break the code. Each glob, scene, section had an essence and I was trying to discover the code, the combination to best deliver that message. In short, I guess I would be looking for Uncle Abner's logic.

The great advantage of the essence method was that it was super-economical, logisticwise cross referencing was almost non-existent and it could be super-accurate. Unfortunately, it could be superdangerous. It was like playing double or nothing, but in extremely fluid situation, only two choices lay open to me—trying to control all the variables completely, Hollywood-style, very expensive and time-consuming plus very sterile, or trying to guide the variables, to wing it, rolling with the punches, keeping the old head above water and steering in the general direction, worrying about details later.

Actually, any dispute about alternatives would have been academic. Not having the bread, nor the time to completely control the variables, you couldn't really even call it a decision; I didn't have a choice. Besides, I figured I had a pretty good chance of making it work, ghetto odds, anyway.

There were two extremely fluid stages in *Sweetback*. Editing was one, but before that there had been the shooting itself, which had involved actors.

I would try to find the grain of the actor just as I would the grain of a scene and if it fitted with the characterization I wanted I would just heighten the real personality and make any extra adjustments externally, with clothing, dialogue, or something else. Beatle, Sweetback's boss, and the woman who takes off Sweetback's handcuffs after he takes care of business provide two examples. In Beatle's bathroom scene, I made Beatle say the dialogue over and over, pretending to be displeased. I would make him keep on going after he had run out of text, then start over again. When I began to see emerging in his performance what I was looking for, I quietly gave the cameras a signal to start shooting (Beatle thought the cameras had been rolling all along) . . . The other bit, the woman in the handcuff scene, worked similarly, but was easier to handle. Since I wanted something lower-keyed. It only took a couple of proddings to get the sister to poke out her mouth and remember back to that chicken-shit brother, whoever he was.

The night club singer made for an entirely different problem. The role was not the actress's real person. I wanted her to explode, but she was normally very well-mannered. By chance, I had an opening three days before she was scheduled to shoot and I called her and asked if I could move her up . . . All right, she would come in, but she was going to Las Vegas for the weekend and had to make a one o'clock plane. I promised her she would have plenty of time to make her plane. Naturally, we were running late when it got to her scene. We started rehearsing; it was good but it could have been better. She asked me what time it was and I got this inspiration and told her it was an hour later than it actually was and that she had missed her mother-fucking plane and that I didn't give a good mother fuck and to get her mother-fucking ass back in there before I put my foot in it. She was so pissed she almost took the guy playing the detective's head off and the scene came out perfectly. (Of course she did the laughing part after her monologue was over and I told her the right time . . . She made the plane too, she told me later.)

The geezer who changes clothes with Sweetback, the girl who seduces the young Sweetback, the detectives and the commissioner are examples of classic full composition acting; that is actors doing their roles.

During the entire shooting, I never had the slightest trouble with any of my cast. Everybody not only did his job but pitched in, just like the crew, anywhere he could give a hand. For example, Detective #1, who is seen at the morgue with the commissioner, was also the real owner of the white dog that was supposed to be the geezer's companion. When the dog refused to run with his movie master, his real master Nick Ferarri put on the costume and ran with the dog so we could get the shot for inter-cutting. The only other actors who had stand-ins, doubles, were the live dogs, who got doubled by two dead dogs I was able to borrow from a humane society. Boy, were we lucky . . . At first, the society didn't even think it could help us . . . but after a little donation, they looked in their refrigerator again, I guess, and found almost exactly what we were searching for . . . There must be a *Reader's Digest* moral in there somewhere about people of the free world working together in the cooperation that has made the country great or something. Notwithstanding all that stuff, I got 100 percent loyalty and 200 percent cooperation. I must admit I regretted the 200 percent cooperation a little the time I got the clap.

I always approach the sex scenes with the most professional of intentions. My partners did too. Besides I still had the normal directing considerations on my mind—framing, sound, general flow, etc. . . . On the other hand, I wanted the love scenes to seem real, so the pretending was pretty close to the real thing. Anyway, T.M.A.L.S.S., the first couple of takes we would be—I think the word is simulating, but then what the hell, you'd start figuring I'm here, she's here, we're here, everybody thinks we ARE . . . you sort of look at each other and you both know and the next take, KERPLUNK. Once though I didn't KERPLUNK. I sure wish that the once that I didn't had been the clap trap instead of the other time.

The fatal morning seemed normal enough until I tried to pee and almost went through the toilet ceiling. It felt like somebody was running a hot sandpaper poker up my thing. I hadn't had so many tears in my eyes since the time I bet about how many chili peppers I could handle, or the time I'd gotten athlete's foot from the high school locker room and someone stepped on my toe as I was rushing to get into homeroom before the bell.

I calculated back and came up with the culpritress. Her hands were clean at least because she had whispered don't and I had whispered back to shut up, that I knew what I was doing. (I still feel she could have put up a bigger struggle, especially when I had to call some other young ladies to warn them about this terrible thing I picked up from this toilet seat, etc. . . . or every time I would get that penicillin needle in my ass.) Ever determined to turn adversity into triumph, I applied for workmen's compensation and got it.

I got 100 percent loyalty and 200 percent cooperation from the crew too, but I didn't catch the clap.

The tingle of fear each time I began a section, like the guy jumping off the tenth floor ledge, looking for the code, the essence, the peaceful solitude . . . Almost regretfully, I watched bit by bit the pieces begin to accumulate . . . I knew the long, wonderful solitary part of the journey was coming to an end.

Then one day all the pieces were edited and there was that last reef to run . . . I spent the next few days assembling all the pieces. Whew! I breathed a sigh of relief. Vulnerability is a mother and at the beginning of pre-pre-production, my production manager had told me I only had sixty-five minutes of story and I had told him he was wrong, but I really didn't know and even after the pieces added up to a couple of hours, I still couldn't believe it and kept checking the arithmetic. But there it was, all assembled, thirteen reels, ten minutes to a reel, one hundred and thirty minutes, two hours and ten minutes. That one remark had haunted me. Two hours and ten minutes. Whew. I had Jerry call the projection room and make a date and we loaded the reels on the dolly and wheeled them down to the screening room to see what God had wrought.

I loved the film. But I began to suspect I was a little less than objective because the projectionist was having trouble with a reel and the images hadn't even started; he had only dimmed the lights.

I squinted my eyes to be critical, I doubled, nay, tripled my efforts, but I loved it anyway.

Now for the seasoning, just like I laid out in my UP-FRONT AIMS PROGRAM. Everything worked. So I had a combination of options and innumerable ways to go about tightening. Even the accordion part, the desert business, the wound, the water, the lizard, between leaving the Mexicans and the rock festival in all scenes I had compromised during the shooting—fitted in as if they had been part of the original glove.

The film had some gems that sparkle brightly and command attention: Bob's photography, Jose's second unit interrogations, the music, maybe even Sweetback's characterization. But for me there were two gems buried deep in its foundation. First, the sound effects which added so much reality to the film, and second, the script. I return to the script once again.

Remember the story about Ulysses tying himself to the mast of his ship to defeat the temptation of the Sirens? Well, the script was my mast and I held on for dear life against the Sirens' songs. Sometimes the temptation was to keep an image that was great in itself but didn't contribute enough to the overall story—or not to shorten a scene that was great but went on too long. Oh the Sirens sang their songs but I held on to the script and pruned away . . . Sometimes it was simply a shtick that had cost me a lot of sweat and blood that had to go. I wasn't going to just FOLLOW the script. I was determined to be TRUE to the script as true as my material allowed. I tightened away. There is nothing to break your heart like those last loving, brilliant, movielens cuts hitting the editing room floor, baby doomed forever. Some people pretend it doesn't bother them and maybe it doesn't, but to me it's like your old gang breaking up or graduation or something.

The sound effects and music were about ready. My two sound editors from *Watermelon Man*, Hans and Luke, were doing the effects for me again. Hans had of course a German accent and Luke sounded like he came out of the second row of a lynch mob, but we got along great. I got along pretty well with all of the technicians. The technician in Hollywood is the nigger, pecking-order-wise, so we related at high gear. (In fact I have this whole theory about Hollywood being a plantation.)

Much of the film was shot silently and so the sound job was immense. Imagine the car explosion without the sound for instance. As "right" as it sounds, the bangs weren't always there; they had to be added. The visual is so much more of an attention-grabbing element in a movie that sound tends to be neglected. Good sound effects tend to be taken for granted and bad sound effects are simply annoying without the viewer being able to pinpoint his discomfort. I dig sound and working semiimpressionistically as I was, I felt precise audio correlation was vital.

Take another example: when Sweetback runs up the steps to the farm where the girls are being prepared for prostitution. Each footstep had to be "cut in" because, once again, the scene had been shot silently. If the sound of his steps were left off, he would seem to be floating. If they were out of sync, he would seem to be stumbling.

In general sound effects are added in two ways, from a library of stock sounds (the car explosions) or at the Foley stage (where the picture is projected on screen and live sound is matched to the image). Even when a scene isn't shot silently, sound effects are often added to beef up the reality and make it appear more normal, for example, the orgy sequence.

Besides using sound "normally" sometimes I used it as a transitional bridge over troubled waters. I had this theory about using sound not in the concrete but in the abstract, to help tell the story, a chore usually reserved for music.

Music-wise, since I wanted an especially tight sound I thought it would be better to get a group used to playing together, rather than a studio orchestra. I met the most together brother—you just never know, do you. It was ex-secretary's boy friend, the one she claimed stopped her from doing the nude part. He had a group that was so out of sight, they didn't laugh at the way I wrote music. They called themselves Earth, Wind & Fire. It was a relief to work with cats I could allow to interpolate for me, knowing that we had an extremely similar frame of reference, especially since following my muse I discovered I was going to be using music to do some dialogue duty too.

Sweetback practically never said a word, but that's just the way he was, I figured. I honestly never thought about it. Then one day when he reaches the desert suddenly I heard him and these voices fussing. I was flabbergasted and like everybody else, when faced with the unexpected, I was frightened. (I suppose, to be honest, I was hostile too. My little package was all neat, not a loose end in sight, and here was shit being thrown in the game.) I didn't want to listen but I knew I was going to.

Who is he arguing with out there in the desert anyway? Is he delirious? My muse, who was peering over my shoulder, said he was rapping with angels.

"Angels?" I asked.

"Angels!" my muse said.

Goddamn—NO SHIT. Now that I thought about it, of course angels, that made all kinds of sense. I never saw any reason to believe that the heaven the Man runs would be any different from good old terra firma. And since an angel was one of God's hand-picked disciples, I knew a blood angel sure had to be jive.

"COLORED angels?"

My muse nodded.

"Buszwah colored angels?"

My muse nodded again, and my muse and I started laughing and he held his palm up and I smacked my palm in his, soul brother-wise. Actually I whacked the side of the Moviola, or that's the way it would have seemed to what they call a casual observer.

No shit, it was so clear to me you dig—that's what they were shouting about. The hand-picked colored house angels mimicking Massa to the bone, liberalism and all, had taken mercy on that poor misguided field nigger Sweetback and they had big-heartedly decided to lay on him the key to obtaining their greatest possession, an honorary white card.

But ass-licking, you dig ain't Sweetback's style no more, he wants to be free, not pseudo-free or one-third-or-so free like the Man used to allow him to be when they used him as an exploitive tool. At last Sweetback has seen the hype.

"If you can't beat 'em, join them," the colored angels counsel. But Sweetback goes on. They begin to plead for him to turn back as colored people do, because each step he goes past the line is an indictment of their "rationality", i.e. their cop out. Just like Rap Brown says, "There's a point where common sense ends and cowardice begins."

Sweetback keeps on keeping on and keeps on keeping on—who says you can't beat 'em in the first place? Slowly something vital begins to return to the soul of the colored-angels: pride, hope and courage, their blackness . . . Sweetback has turned them around!

"Run, Sweetback . . . Run, mother fucker," they shout, letting it hang out.

That was it! I knew it was right! It was so right I never even had to make a change in my neat little package I had gotten so possessive and orderly and buszwah about until my muse pulled my ass up short. It was as if I had been working toward that point all along and didn't even know it.

The next to last stage in a film before you get a finished print is called dubbing. You take all the non-visual elements-dialogue, sound effects and music—and mix them together on the dubbing stage and send that band along with the images to the lab and get back a composite print (a print composed of sound and images together). Before dubbing, everything has to be gone over and checked, every element and every piece of element. Stuff you just KNEW was right had to be gone over and over.

Fatigue was beginning to get to me, I was barely making it, and Jerry was already half-dead. Each morning he stumbled in later and later.

One thing the worm and Lady Luck have in common is they do turn. *Watermelon Man* was doing well. I didn't read the *Variety* box office score-board, I just read the grins and bows that began to blossom in my path and the "Hi, Mels, how're you doing?" and I could tell the attendance figure, give or take a hundred seats. In the meantime, all the major studios, Columbia included, were trying harder and harder to lure independent filmmakers into using their facilities as I was doing.

Things were a long way from a bed of roses—but it beat the post office. But then again, almost anything beat the post office. As if the tedium shit and exhaustion weren't enough, I had a couple of other minuses singeing my ass. Dubbing is very expensive and I didn't have the bread, plus the unions were on my case again. Not only were they already down on me, but I wanted them to give me the union seal of approval so I could get the film shown in any theater in the U.S.

So I took my two pluses and my three minuses and did me some ghetto arithmetic and got myself a plus one. Since then some pseudo-intellectual brother pointed out to me that a minus three and a plus two don't equal a plus one. Well, it was my turn and I pointed out to the dumb mother fucker he just really didn't understand the power of positive block-thinking.

I went to Columbia and apologized about the union problems I had created through my ignorance and offered to use union people when I dubbed. In fact, I noticed their dubbing stage was empty . . . but then again I didn't want to impose on them because I PREFERRED not to pay cash . . . (that was quite all right . . . all right . . . your credit chuckle is good Mel . . . saw the figures on *Watermelon Man* it's looking pretty good isn't it chuckle) . . . Of course I wanted to be sure I got the union seal as I would if I mixed at another studio . . . (sure thing Mel . . . sure thing chuckle) . . . Could I have that in writing please so YOU are protected . . . (sure thing Mel . . . sure thing, be in the mail this afternoon . . . Always a pleasure doing business with you, Mel old pal) . . . ditto . . . always a pleasure doing business with you guys.

On a Tuesday morning a couple of weeks before dubbing was to begin, Jerry came in and announced that he needed a rest and was quitting.

I hit him in the mouth and grabbed his hair and throw him down. Every time he tried to explain, I hit his head on the floor.

"Listen, mother fucker, don't be coming in here and telling me what you GONNA DO . . .

"But . . ."

(Whack) I bounced his head off the floor. "You gonna leave this Goddamn film when I LET you."

"But" . . .

(Whack) I bounced his head off the floor. "If you try and cross me again I'll pull your asshole out through your eye socket . . ."

"Please let me up."

I let him up but some people learn very slowly. As soon as he got on his feet he tried to start discussing again and so I whopped him upside his head a couple of more times. (Whack, Whack!)

"Look mother fucker we made a deal and you're the only one who knows these elements besides me and if I don't have this film ready soon and pick up some bread I'm gonna lose my head . . . you know what mother fucker its gonna be your ass before mine I'll personally see to that."

Jerry got back on the ball and I got 100 percent loyalty and 200 percent cooperation to the end of the film.

The day dubbing was to begin was like the day the circus was coming to town or Christmas morning, one of those things that weren't ever going to happen. But like the other never moments, it finally came.

For the hell of it we all decided that we would dress up for the occasion. Jerry had on a double-breasted jacket and a patterned ascot like old-time movie people wore and some tennis shoes he had dyed purple. I had on my navy blue Nehru that a guy had given me when the Nehru style went out and a striped tie. Luke had on a dark suit and Hans had forgotten that we had decided to put on the dog and had on his usual leather sports jacket, but he always looked impeccable so it didn't matter about him.

We walked on to the dubbing platform standing tall. We had our shit together and we knew we had our shit together. I sat in the raised director's chair facing the large silver screen at the far end of the room. Directly in front of me ten feet or so was the mixing panel, a huge array of lights and switches as wide across as a normal room. It looked like the control panel of a spaceship from tomorrow. Three mixers were seated at the controls, music to my left, dialogue in the middle and sound effects on my right. Hans, Luke and Jerry stood behind me. The green light came on and the music mixer's hand went to the start button. He turned and looked at me for confirmation.

"O.K. Let's do it," I said.

The room went black and I thought about everything that had gone down, especially a traveling shot of a white pipe suspended across a ravine by two huge pylons, the last cut that I had taken out . . . I threw it out of my mind . . . The film started . . . besides, to remember is to mourn.

We went to work and four days later we had finished dubbing. I tried to look humble but there was no holding my man the muse who strutted around and right-on'd his ass off.

Since I had cut the negative as I went, five days after dubbing was over I had my composite print and the film was finished.

It don't matter if you burn everybody for the first 99 percent of a race, it's the whole 100 percent that counts. Brothers and sisters have been programmed to stop short of the finish line. Just do your thing the Man tells you while he grabs ownership, power and bread. . . . Fuck that. In short, the film was finished but I wasn't.

I was determined to keep that possession, being nine-tenths up-tight. Having a percentage in a movie is supposed to be very complicated. There are so many ways to cut the cake. It isn't complicated worth a mother fuck if you don't cut the cake.

I had offers from majors but they just wanted to give me the prestige of THEIR taking a chance with me. Fuck that in

I wanted bread and control. In the end I LEASED the film to a smaller company called Cinemation Industries because I liked the style of Gross, the boss, and especially his second, Marenstein. They had balls and brains, enough brains in fact to know they didn't know black folks and that's pretty smart for white men.

I had this theory about a really synchronized movie and music tie-up, so I prepared an album and took the masters to Stax Records and made a deal with them.

I gave a screening to try the film out on an audience. After the movie these three fine sisters came out and started hugging me and telling me how great it was to see a brother getting it on for once and how proud they were and how they loved that shot of Sweetback standing there with the hat on digging Beatle and the two detectives. They said at that moment, they would have done anything Sweetback asked. Well, you don't have to hit me over the head with a sledgehammer. The Lord had given me a sign and I used that shot as the symbol of the film . . . I have never regretted it.

In the meantime, the Motion Picture Association and I were hassling because I maintained white folks had no right to judge films for black folks. I started suing them. The very first rule of the block is don't write no check with your mouth your ass can't cash. I'm sure glad I wasn't depending on the Negro media to help me cash my check because most of the colored papers started some luke-warm shit about me first having to prove myself to them. One even called the suit a publicity stunt just like *Variety*, the show biz newspaper, had. In fact, the blood couldn't even write his own copy. He just changed the order of a couple of sentences . . . Niggers can sure be discouraging sometimes.

We were all ready to go. All set . . . except for one little thing. There isn't a black-owned movie chain in America, not even a Negro or a colored one, and all the theaters except two refused to book the picture. Only two theaters in the entire country willing to play the film. But the Man has an Achilles pocket book and I knew if the film did well all the doors would swing wide. But if the picture bombed for ANY reason, external or not, from an earthquake on down . . . In short, if I didn't come up with a presentable gross I was dead—typical odds, ghetto-wise . . . FUCK IT . . . OPEN IT.

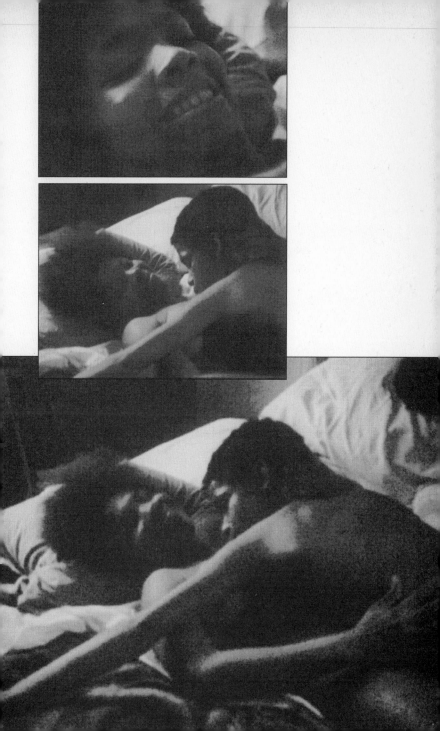

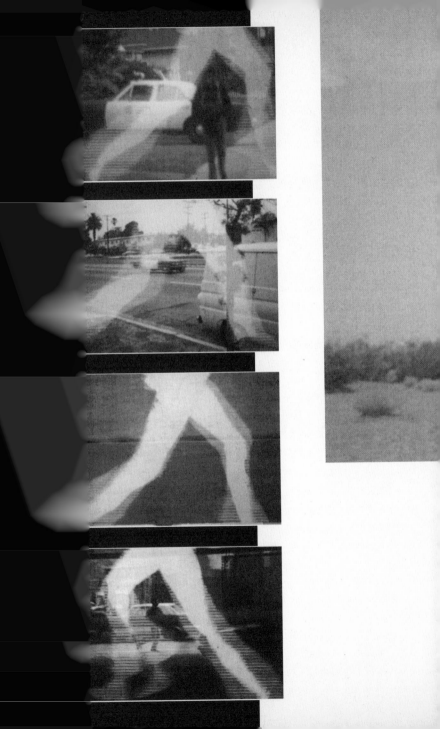

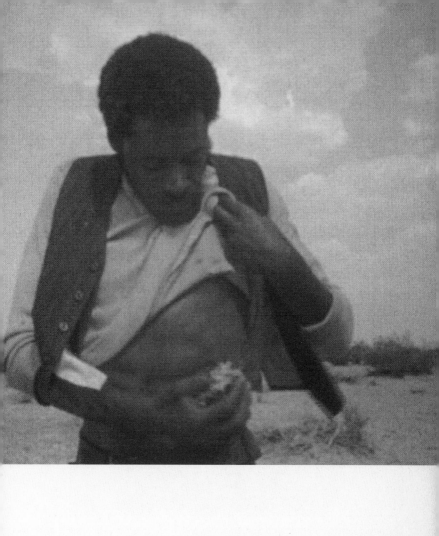

WATCH OUT

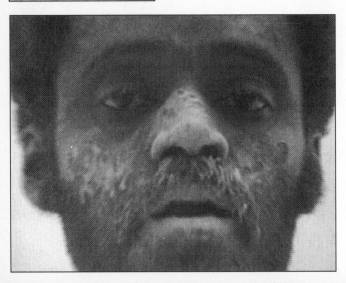

A BAAD ASSSSS NIGGER IS COMING BACK
TO COLLECT SOME DUES...

SHOOTING SCRIPT

MARCH 6, 1970, 6:20 P.M. L.A.

Women lined up like sort of a feminine wild bunch, standing in a semicircle around a kitchen table. They are half undressed or rather dressed in housecoats, the classic garment of their profession. The time is middle World War II, circa 1943–44. Each whore is gazing downward with a shy almost maternal look on her face. There is slurping, smacking, grunting noise and the camera pans downward. A filthy, half-starved nappy headed boy is hunched over the kitchen table gobbling food from his plate at an incredible pace, as if eating were going out of style. He steals fugitive glances up from his plate as if he fears being struck or his food taken away, but the eating never slows. One of the women brings the pot from the stove and refills his plate. The women nod and smile warmly at one another.

One of the whores, fortyish, is washing herself from her basin, half squatting and half standing, with one leg propped on the rung of a chair. The door is ajar and the boy, the same one who was at the kitchen table but now cleaned up and healthy looking, walks past with a load of towels. The woman goes to the door. The hall is empty except for the boy. She calls him. When he enters the room she is standing by the bed. She signals him to come toward her, she takes off her robe and lies back on the bed waiting. The boy comes to the edge of the bed. She sits up and starts to unbutton his shirt. She nods at him reassuringly. The boy undresses. She wraps herself around him and lays back on the bed, pulling him on top of her. She adjusts him in her, looking at him with warmth and mischieviousness.

He lays there immobile.

Pause . . .

The boy is still immobile.

"This ain't the photographer's . . . you ain't here to get your picture taken," the woman says. ". . . Move."

Pause . . . and then the boy's back begins to move. Intercutting between the boy's back and her face. At first she whispers instructions but the boy is a natural. Her expression changes to surprise, then to intensity all the time the back is going. Then her expression changes to ecstasy and total surrendering. She screams . . .

"Oh God," her scream echoes through the house. "Oh God son," she moans, "you got a sweetback . . . a sweet, sweetback," and then the main title flashes on:

SWEET SWEETBACK'S BAADAASSSSS SONG

The credits continue, superimposed over a montage of shots of Sweetback's back pumping, women's faces, and Sweetback's legs running.

When the titles finish, we are in the present. A freak show is going on in the living room. A dingy red carpet has been placed in the center of the room to imply a stage, and strangely enough, it works. We have the impression we are watching theatre, not as it is now, but as it once might have been, a morality play or something like that out of the Middle Ages.

In the room across the hall the boss of the house, a short, grotesque very black man called Beatle, is arguing with two white plainclothesmen, arguing that is, as much as a black man operating outside the law can argue with white men supposedly representing the law, which isn't, of course, very much. There was a disturbance out in front of Beatle's the night before and some corpse had the inconsideration to be found on his doorstep. It is the beat of the two white detectives and they are supposed to be conducting an investigation. Fortunately, the corpse had been a black man. The plainclothesmen know the whole thing will quickly blow over . . . yet still, keeping abreast of the times, at least a show of concern had to be made for the poor departed brother.

They tell Beatle they need someone to go down to the station for appearance sake and at least spend a night in the jail.

Beatle complains that he is short of help and only has two men working at the moment to keep the girls in line plus do everything else . . . Donald to explain and Sweetback to train and the two of them to count bounce and trounce.

Meanwhile, across the hall in the living room, the pageant play unfolds. A lesbian picks up a girl on a bench. They walk in the park. The lesbian persuades the girl to go up to her room and they make love. The exhausted girl finally falls asleep, the lesbian rolls from beside the girl, she kneels on the dingy carpet. She holds her hands and begins to pray. The lights go off in the living room. Some of the women spectators squeal. Then something appears in the center of the stage spotted with a flashlight. It sports an outlandish costume, a white frilly dress, perhaps from some long-ago ball or wedding, a garland of plastic flowers on its head, cardboard wings and a Fourth of July sparkler as a wand. It turns full circle.

"I am the Good Dyke Fairy Godmother," it announces. It turns full circle again and then goes over and touches the lesbian with the wand and the lesbian turns into a man and stands up. The people lean forward applauding and the lights come back on. The ex-lesbian awakens the girl. The girl is overjoyed at the transformation and they make love once again.

"Now Sweetback here is the greatest," the Good Dyke Fairy Godmother announces, pointing to the man alias lesbian. "The absolute greatest . . . I know what you are thinking ladies and gentlemen, especially you girls . . . Ha, Ha, Ha. How many times have I heard that before . . . well, as a special added attraction, if one of you ladies would like to step up and try the gentleman, I'm sure he'll be more than lively . . . cause this here Good Dyke Fairy Godmother only transforms into Number One material."

Even though the cops have seen the number a thousand times, they always end up drifting across the hall standing in the living room doorway trying to look casual.

A skinny white girl, itching to take advantage of the Good Dyke Fairy Godmother's offer starts to get up but her date pulls her back in her seat. She snatches her arm away and starts to get up again. The Good Dyke Fairy Godmother catches the frozen expressions on the white cops faces and deftly saves the situation.

"Of course, you know . . . that is . . . er . . . it goes without saying that this offer is only open to sisters . . ."

The white cops burst into smiles and the skinny white girl sits down visibly disappointed. The cops tell Beatle to make up his mind because they have to take someone. He wouldn't want a real investigation, would he. Beatle sighs and then gives an order to one of the girls.

"As soon as Sweetback is finished, tell him to get dressed and that I want to see him."

Finally Sweetback appears. He is sharply dressed, sharp as a rat turd as the expression goes, a rat turd having the distinction of being pointed on both ends. His outfit pinpoints his status exactly. Pink shirt with an enormous collar, black pants and vest, cream-colored sports jacket, topped off with a black felt copy of a banana plantation overseer's straw sombrero, in short, a young up and coming small-time big shot. His clothes fit beautifully but the expression on his face seems out of place. Something about him makes people uneasy. It's impossible to be sure what his stare hides. Some would say intelligence, some would say sensuality, some say stupidity, some meanness. Anyway, everyone's first thought is to try to get on his good side.

"Go with these gentlemen for the evening," Beatle says.

Sweetback follows the two detectives without a word.

One detective drives and the other detective and Sweetback climb in the back.

"We aren't going to use the handcuffs," the detective driving says through the grill separating him from the back. "Like we told Beatle it's just a little eyewash."

The detective sitting next to Sweetback grins in agreement and offers Sweetback a cigarette. Sweetback shakes his head. They drive through the night. Suddenly the radio breaks the silence. A shoot-out has begun between a patrol and some militants. The two plainclothesmen are the first reinforcements to arrive on the scene. They part around the corner from the battle. They handcuff Sweetback to the grill and rush toward the action. Sweetback can hear shooting but he can't see what is going on.

A few moments later a policeman in uniform and the two plainclothesmen dash from around the corner with a young black prisoner in tow.

"I think he must be the ringleader," the policeman pants. "They tried to lay down a covering fire for him to escape."

"Let's get him out of here before the crowd forms."

One of the plainclothesmen slams the young man, Moo-Moo, in the back seat next to Sweetback and gets in back again himself. He unhitches Sweetback from the grill and handcuffs him to Moo-Moo instead. The other plainclothesman gets in the driver's seat and they skid away from the curb.

But they don't drive directly to the station.

In South Los Angeles, there are a series of pumps that have been beautified up in the interest of civic mindness to resemble grasshoppers. Big plastic eyes, the size of Volkswagen hubcaps have been fastened on the head and steel rods have been welded on for antennas. The cops pull behind the most secluded grasshopper pump.

They slap Moo-Moo, they pull him from the car and begin to beat him. They can't beat him too well because he and Sweetback are shackled together. They apologize to Sweetback for the inconvenience. They unleash Moo-Moo so they can beat him better. They begin to work Moo-Moo over in earnest. The grasshopper pump bobs up and down grinning and staring evilly. Sweetback stands quietly back with his arms at his sides and the empty handcuff dangles from his wrist. Suddenly the pattern of Sweetback's destiny changes. The cops have their backs to him. He gazes at them bending over the boy working him over. He attacks the cops, using the free handcuff as a pair of lethal brass knuckles. He is so swift and sure they never even realize what hit them. They fall unconscious and he still beats them, his blows rise and fall in time with the Grasshopper pump, again and again and again.

He drags the semi-conscious Moo-Moo away and bathes his face in a nearby creek. Moo-Moo tries to express his gratitude. Sweetback is his old noncommittal self. They split the scene and then divide up and head in different directions.

Near noon the next day, a raiding party of cops charge through the corridor of Beatle's Brothel. For the occupants it is the middle of the night, everyone had been asleep. The whores scream as the cops bust into the rooms searching. The last room they come in is Beatle's. Beatle is asleep with a cat in one arm and a rabbit in the other and a stocking cap on his head. Beatle sits up in an obviously innocent and surprised manner, as a black man can.

Waves going in and out, going in and out. Just like the song. Sweetback is sitting on the deck of the Santa Monica pier. His coat is draped casually over his right arm and down over his wrist hiding his handcuffs. The waves keep coming and going and time passes. Night begins to fall. Sweetback thinks about the ghetto. He watches the merry-go-round, he walks along the beach, it gets dark and cold. Some kids build a fire.

Beatle's place. Sweetback has been watching the house

for the right moment. The last customer lurches away in the dawn's early light and Sweetback goes inside. Beatle says he is very glad to see Sweetback and talks about business necessities, public relations, how they must all stick together and that it will all blow over in a few days and that Sweetback should go out by the back door. Sweetback steps out on the back porch and starts down the steps, two cops with their guns drawn grab him and march him over to a corner of the yard.

The cops still handle Sweetback kindly, almost apologetically. The two plainclothesmen Sweetback jumped and beat in back of the pump are still in comas and haven't talked yet. Everyone assumes Sweetback was more or less an innocent bystander to Moo-Moo's attack and escape. But then the cops see the handcuffs dangling from his wrist, their minds flash to the wounds on the plainclothesmen and they begin to put two and two together . . .

A few moments later: the commissioner's office is full of reporters. The phone rings. The commissioner listens, then says, "Oh yes, I see you have the witness called 'Sweetback' and you say Mr. Sweetback knows the whereabouts of the suspect but that Mr. Sweetback had been injured in a fall? Not too badly I hope." The commissioner speaks slowly and distinct as if he were dictating and the reporters jot down what he says.

"Can we print this Commissioner?" one of the reporters asks.

"Of course," the commissioner says. "I have no secrets from the press."

The cop on the other end of the line sitting in the police car in front of Beatle's is thoroughly confused and to add to his trouble two black kids with pails are trying to wash his car. They begin to pour something they say is a special cleaner over the hood.

"If you don't like it, Mister, you don't have to pay," one of the kids assures him.

The cops sigh in resignation. He has more important problems than panhandling pickaninnies. What the hell is the commissioner talking about. The cop tries to explain again but the commissioner interrupts him.

"Fine, fine," the commissioner says. "You say the witness has given you the whereabouts of the suspect? Too bad the witness bruised himself in a fall . . . proceed."

Finally the cop begins to get the message. The first cop comes back from the car telephone. The other cop has handcuffed Sweetback's wrists together and has his police special trained on him.

"Well," the second cop asks.

"Commissioner wants us to whip the information out of this nigger before we bring him to the station."

They begin to work Sweetback over. Sweetback doesn't utter a sound.

"Let's go someplace where we can really get to work on this guy."

They half drag, half push Sweetback to the patrol car. The cop reaches into his pocket to give the two boys some change for their troubles but they run off. They push Sweetback in the car and hop in. The driver cop slams the door and the car bursts into a ball of flame.

The second cop jumps out of the back seat with Sweetback but the driver cop's door is jammed.

Sweetback escapes in the confusion.

Livid with rage, the police commissioner pulls down a wall map of the ghetto and glares at it.

Banging on a door, *a woman* pulls up the shade. She has obviously been sleeping. She stares out and quickly opens the door, Sweetback comes in. In the semi-darkness she doesn't notice Sweetback's battered state or the handcuffs. She immediately lights into him.

"You sure are jive . . . now don't come tellin' me you're looking for Steve cause you know Steve ain't here. He got two more months to go." Sweetback doesn't answer.

"Are you some kind of Indian Giver or something . . . you gave me to him. Now here you come back begging . . . well, it's just . . ."

Sweetback holds the handcuffs in front of her face and she stops abruptly.

"You want me to get them off?" she says. Sweetback holds the handcuffs closer to her.

"Beg," she says.

"Naw," he says, speaking for the first time.

"You too proud to beg?"

"Naw, but you wouldn't get me out of these things if I did." The woman looks at him for what seems an eternity.

"You know every goddam thing, don't you?" she says. And she pulls her nightgown over her head and lays back on the bed. "First things first," she says. Sweetback moves toward the bed.

Beatle's face more grotesque than ever. His eyes seem as if they are going to pop out of his head. Sweat is pouring from his forehead and he looks as if he has been crying and is going to cry again any minute. His bedroom is a shambles and three detectives are grilling him. One has him by the collar and the other two are on either side. He swears to them he doesn't know where Sweetback is and they keep repeating the question. Seems like he must be a little hard of hearing one cop says to the other. If he don't talk he is gonna be. Where is Sweetback, the cops ask. Beatle says he doesn't know. The cop puts the chamber of his pistol near Beatle's ears and fires a shot into the ceiling. The question is repeated but it seems only half as loud. Beatle's face is distended with pain, a trickle of blood is running from his nose. The cop puts the chamber to the other ear and fires and everything goes quiet.

Sweetback comes into the side entrance of the church off the alley, it was once a shoe repair shop, the old sign is still hanging, announcing HEELS WHILE YOU WAIT. He stands in the shadows looking into the front room. A minister is preaching a funeral service to four old women and six tough looking young blacks.

"Our brother here died today of an overdose. An overdose of misery of black life." One of the women answers with a howl of sorrow.

Sweetback taps on the partition. He stays back in the shadows.

The preacher continues to preach, "Yes Lord . . . Black Misery."

Sweetback taps again. The minister hears the noise.

"We will bow our heads to pray for an expensive future for the cheap body lying in the cheap casket." The minister steps back into the shadows. He sees Sweetback.

"What're you doing Sweetback, they're looking for you. You're as hot as little Sis's twat."

Sweetback is halfway up the back stairs, the minister runs after him.

"Where you going?"

"I want you to cover for me. I'm going upstairs to the farm."

"To the farm? You can't hide there."

"That's the last place Beatle would tell them about . . . the farm is his best supplier of girls," Sweetback says. The minister looks at him and sighs.

"They already know about the farm. And not just yesterday . . . the man knows every move we make."

Sweetback stands with the door of the farm ajar. The sign above the entrance reads HAVEN FOR UNWED MOTHERS. Through the door we can see one side of the room with five or six cots with young women lying on them, some pregnant, some with small children.

"That's it," the minister says. "Oh they don't ever bother me. The hype I'm laying down to these people downstairs ain't dangerous . . . I'm just selling a little bit of happy land. Ain't it strange how our folks rejoice when we die. We don't hurry to die but when we die, the living rejoice. You know why they rejoice . . . they believe that maybe it will be better on the other side. It's my job to make them believe that it's true . . . But Moo-Moo, the boy you saved and them other kids are laying down the real religion. Later for waiting they say. You offer pretty good news to me slapping up on some white cops . . . I'm going to say a Black Ave Maria for you . . . That's the real flower, get it now like them kids say, later for waiting. And that's why the man's down on you. You saved Moo-Moo . . . you saved a plant they was planning on nippin' in the bud . . .

Gotta go on and give him some happy, happy about the never, never land." The minister turns and goes down the steps. Over his shoulder he says, "I'm gonna still say a couple of Black Ave Marias for you."

"What does a dead man need bread for," the manager's talking to Sweetback. It's night and we're in a room, a sleazy little gambling place. Under the huge masked lamps there are four or five men sitting hunched over their cards.

"So they was whipping a brother and how about the brothers you whipped and the sisters you slipped. Life's tough baby . . . struggle from the womb to the tomb. Every dollar we make the guineas get 40 cents and the cops get 50 cents and Goldberg gets 20 cents. And that equals a dollar and a dime and that's why us niggers are always in debt for that dime. I haven't forgot you staked me Sweetback. If I had the bread I'd lay it on you. But I just don't have it . . . Anyhow, like I say, why does a dead man need bread."

"And Mother Africa reaches out her black arms," one of the card players looks up and says. He pauses and looks around the table, "and pulls back a bloody stump."

"You can't leave this town by wings, wheel or steel, Sweetback," the manager says. "I wouldn't shuffle or shit you."

The manager, Sweetback and Big Henry, the manager's bodyguard, drive through the city. The Greyhound bus station is swarming with plainclothesmen trying to look innocuous, surveying all of the black men buying tickets.

"Just like the rail station," Big Henry says and they pull away from the curb.

"Stop, " Sweetback says. And leaps out of the car and runs toward someone who starts to retreat, then stops. It's Moo-Moo.

"Moo-Moo brothers," Moo-Moo says, extending his hand to the manager and Big Henry. They simply nod.

The car rolls along. It seems to be heading out of the city. It begins to rain.

"You got my partner in a parcel of trouble," the manager says.

"Where are you taking us?" Moo-Moo says.

They don't answer immediately. They simply drive on in the downpour. They turn off on a small road.

"This is the best I can do for you on such short notice," the manager says, opening the door for Sweetback and Moo-Moo. Big Henry has pulled his gun out just in case they disagree. Sweetback and Moo-Moo get out and stand in the downpour. Sweetback's old buddy pulls some bills off his wad and stuffs them into Sweetback's jacket pocket.

"Buy yourself a last supper . . . you're dead," the manager says. The car backs up, turns around and skids off into the night.

They are nowhere. They begin to walk down the road. They discover an abandoned building that was probably a power station or small factory. Scattered here and there on the dirt floor, there are still indentations where pieces of heavy machinery must have stood.

Sweetback dreams. He dreams about breaking into stores for cigarettes. He dreams about all the lights turned on him throughout his life from interrogations to . . . he wakes . . . a gigantic flashlight is shining directly in his eyes and there is a powerful roar.

It isn't a flashlight at all. It's a headlight. They have stumbled into a motorcycle gang's den. The gang says they are trespassing and since that is a no-no, they gotta pay. But then maybe since they didn't know, they are being a little harsh on them, one of the gang argues. Yeah, maybe so another one agrees. It is obviously a routine the cycle guys have pulled before, Sweetback tries to figure out where they are headed. Hey, why not duel like they used to do in the old days. With who? With the chief, between this guy and the chief when he gets here. A pack of motorcycles roar down the road like the hounds of hell.

"Relax," they say and they feed Sweetback and Moo-Moo. Later there is a roar of the other cycles arriving and the big door is flung open. The chief and eight or nine other members ride in.

The chief is enormous, six feet something and over three hundred pounds. The chief is a woman. She strides over to Sweetback and sizes him up.

"What are the weapons gonna be," she says. They tell her he hasn't chosen them yet. Knives? She holds out her hands and one of the members hands her a knife. She throws it and it sticks two or three inches into the oak post. Wrestling? She swaggers over to a big bike and lifts it off the ground.

"Well! What do you choose?" she says.

"He does the choosing?" Moo-Moo asks.

"Yep."

"Fucking," Sweetback says.

Silence. The water drips off the roof. One guy starts about no black cat, but another member tells him to shut up . . . a joker says they ain't really got the same weapons. Big Sadie signals for silence.

"Okay," she says, "fucking," and that settles that. Pandemonium breaks loose. The bikes are arranged in a circle with their headlights pointing in the middle. Some of the gang lay their leather jackets in the arena. Some drive their cycles up on a loading ramp and turn the headlights toward the center, too. *Once Big Sadie let ten of the guys pull a train on her and she didn't bat an eyelash* one of the girls tells another one. *You really jumped from the frying pan into the fire, Buddy.*

"Ta ra ta ta de ta," the joker imitates a fanfare.

Big Sadie steps into the ring of light stark naked. She clasps her hands above her head doing the fighter victory thing. The gang members roar their encouragement. Sweetback is shoved into the ring. He is naked too, except for a black derby someone has stuck on his head and a pair of spats fastened around his ankles. He looks like a refugee from an old Tarzan comic strip. Everyone bursts out laughing.

They meet in the center of the arena. Big Sadie laughing and winking at her followers, she lays down on the jackets, folds her arms behind her head and open her legs.

"Well," she smirks.

Sweetback starts to work. Big Sadie's smirk disappears . . . Then her arms come from behind her head . . . Then she begins to hug him. In short, Sweetback begins to make a believer of her. She begins to moan with pleasure, a rumbling roar begins to form in her throat. This dance of life transcends all the frontiers of time, place, color. The spectators are locked with them as if they themselves were writhing on the floor. They begin to cheer them on. Suddenly Big Sadie bellows and begins to scream with pleasure.

Sweetback stands up the winner. Big Sadie lays there almost beautiful and suddenly shy.

Sweetback and Moo-Moo are taken down the road to a combination bar-pool hall closed for the season. The gang breaks the lock and tells them to go inside and wait there. The electricity hasn't been shut off so Sweetback and Moo-Moo play pool to pass the time.

Two white cops walk in on them as Moo-Moo is racking the balls for a new game. A fight ensues . . . Moo-Moo is wounded and one policeman is dead, the other policeman charges Sweetback who spears him with a pool cue.

Sweetback helps Moo-Moo to his feet and they start for the door. There is the sound of a motorcycle. It is a guy from a black motorcycle club that Big Sadie called for help when she overheard the double cross. The guy can't carry two and Big Sadie told him to save Sweetback, but Sweetback makes him take Moo-Moo. He helps Moo-Moo on the back of the bike and the cycle starts off, Moo-Moo is so faint, he falls off. The next time they strap him on. The cycle roars off again. Sweetback ducks into the underbrush and starts running.

The lights in the pool hall are still on and the dead cops stare up at the bulbs like they are going through some eternal interrogations.

NIGHT Sweetback running, running. There are oil pumps in the background.

DAY "I want them and I want them now," the commissioner says. He is addressing a roomful of plain-clothesmen and uniformed cops. He stamps out his cigar in rage. "Cop-killers and niggers to boot. We can have an

uprising on our hands. No patrol will be safe in their area
. . . That's all!" The police begin to file out. He motions to
the Negro patrolmen in the audience to wait behind and
he tells them that he meant no offense with the use of the
word 'Nigger,' just a colloquialism and it would be a great
credit to their people if they capture . . . er them.

DAY Sweetback is catching his breath. He is sitting
under a bridge in the huge "O" formed by a drainpipe.

DAY The cops dash up the outside steps of a motel. The
clerk lets them in. A man and a woman are in bed. The
cops swoop down on the man so rapidly he gets kicked
and slapped ten times before God even gets the news. But
it isn't Sweetback, it's a mistake.

NIGHT Sweetback running through a back street.

NIGHT A police car cruising down a busy, blaring black
business block, a parade, a guy borrowing out of a car, a
barbecue palace.

NIGHT Sweetback jumps over a fence towards the
camera.

NIGHT The door of the commissioner's office opens. A
detective leans in toward the camera and gives the thumbs
up victory sign. The commissioner leaps up from his desk,
his jacket is off and the gun in his shoulder holster looks
enormous.

NIGHT The commissioner's mouth is moving, he is
talking but there is no sound. It looks like he is standing
in a bank vault with a wall of enormous safety deposit
boxes behind him—it's the City Morgue. He looks down.
The camera follows. A drawer is being closed and there is
a glimpse of a cadaver that could be Moo-Moo's. The
attendant starts to pull out another drawer. The camera

looks directly into the commissioner's face again, he is asking something but still there is no sound.

"I ain't learned to read lips yet," Beatle's voice says and we see Beatle in a wheel chair with his man, Donald, standing behind him. His ears are bandaged. Donald, with as much sarcasm in his voice as he dares, tells the commissioner Beatle has lost his hearing. The commissioner writes the question out. IS THIS SWEETBACK? Beatle looks into the drawer. He begins to smile. It is the black guy who was on the motorcycle.

DAY A ravaged, ruthless face bouncing around, a wino dancing on a corner in skid row for the tourists and at the same time being questioned by the police. No sirree he don't know nothing his head swivels back and forth between the camera and his audience, gums flashing. No sirree never heard of no Sweetback. Another ravaged face, a filthy basement an old gnarled woman is cracking string beans into a beat-up pot and filthy half-naked children crawl around in the mess on the concrete. She just keeps the kids for the county after they get so bad or so grown they just takes 'em away, maybe she did keep a Leroy but she can't rightly remember. Another face so heavily painted it looks like it's on its way to be in a Japanese play, fags sitting at a lunch counter, no child . . . I mean officer . . . I am not familiar with a Mr. Sweetback. All the other fags nod in unison. I'm a queen but I'm militant. Another pops in about their rights and the Joker in the crowd asks won't she do they all giggle.

TWILIGHT Sweetback climbs out of a junk yard and starts running.

NIGHT A savage-faced woman yells into a mike then a funky dressing room where you can almost smell the armpits and hair grease, she's been out of trade for years and off the stuff swear to God. The woman gets hysterical and pulls off her costume, there ain't no marks, right! "And she ain't seen that jive ass Sweetback and whenever will be too soon." The savage-faced woman screaming into the mike again and different colored lights are flashing behind her.

NIGHT Rain and trees bending, Sweetback is trying to hitch a ride a sports car zips past him and then the flashing light of a police car making a pinch looms out of the darkness. Sweetback dives behind the shoulder of the road.

NIGHT The commissioner is unshaven he looks obsessed. "Fuck the reporters," he screams. "I know they're out there." He points to a map of Southern California and puts his finger on Mexico. "That's his only prayer so he's got to try for it!"

In the old seat of the pants flying days pilots would fly down from up at the state capital in Sacramento all the way to Ensenada in Baja, Mexico without a map just using the railroad as a running landmark. Even from 500 feet up it stuck out like a sore thumb, but now sometimes at five yards the tracks are unnoticeable; in the city overpowered by freeways and cars and skyscrapers, in the country weather-beaten right back into the landscape, rotting ties and waiting stations crumbled into genteel dilapidation. But anyway, rusting and maybe not so shiny anymore, the rails are still there pointing the way to Mexico.

DAY Sweetback seen from the overpass running down the track, Sweetback on all fours scrambling past a settlement, Sweetback running through the desert along side of the railroad track. He looks over his shoulder and his look becomes . . .

DAY A black guy shining shoes. He puts the polish on and then turns around and wipes the toes with his ass everybody grins. He turns back around and starts his rag to popping. The slap, slap, slap of the rag becomes . . .

DAY The flap, flap, flap of the rotor of a helicopter, there is something running down below in the desert with a dog at its side. Through the windshield of a police car. In the distance a man running with a dog loping at his side. A warning shot is fired, the man squatted down in the sage and sand. He is so browned he is maybe even part Negro, maybe Indian. The man pats the dog. The sheriff questions him.

"Why did you run?"

"How come I run? I ran cause I keep my word."

"What word?"

"I promised to run."

"Promised."

"Promised this guy who gave me five dollars . . . promised to run if some people came after me."

"Black guy?"

"Yeah. Colored."

"What did he look like?"

"Like a buddy I used to pal around with in Denver."

"So tall? About this size?" The sheriff indicates Sweetback's height.

"Yeah, about that I'd say."

DAY Sweetback riding along in a pickup truck full of Mexican workers. Everybody is eating, Sweetback too. The truck turns off onto another road and stops. Sweetback jumps down. We are still in the States. The road sign is in English. The Mexican points off in the distance and the truck pulls away everybody waves.

DAY Sweetback is running. There is the sound of a scout plane overhead. Sweetback makes it to a clump of trees he is winded. The plane seems to recede. When Sweetback leaves the trees the plane appears on the horizon again and zooms overhead and becomes a car with two sheriffs deputies in uniform and a member of a civilian posse wearing a star and a plaid shirt. Seen from above the sheriff's car speeding down the road with a wake of dust it could almost be a shot of Rommel rushing to the front in a war movie. The car overtakes someone walking down the road blasts its horn for room. More and more people are on the road. The car goes through horns tooting. Kids, everywhere moving along the road, in the background the sheriffs car surrounded by kids has had to slow down to a snail's pace, it's a youth army heading for a rock festival.

DAY As kids freak out cops are converging on the area passing in and out among the youths searching, searching. From the bandstand bass guitar chords are underlying the search for Sweetback. Every now and then in the distance a policeman runs over to someone, other cops join him then they disperse again and continue their search.

NIGHT The lights come on at the festival. Suddenly Sweetback and a cop see one another. Sweetback looks around and starts walking for a clump of bushes he overtakes a black girl dressed in African style and starts to put his arm around her. The cop runs over and gets another cop and tells him he swears he has seen Sweetback. Where, over there in that clump of bushes. They draw their guns, it sure looks suspicious the bandstand is that way and you say he ran that way. They sneak upon the bushes . . . they part the bushes and look down. They burst out laughing. All they see is a black guy and girl making love. The cops begin to laugh they don't see the knife Sweetback is holding against the girl's ribs. Well I guess I would be in a rush too they say and they laugh again and walk off.

NIGHT Sweetback running through the trees. Sweetback running through a field overhead the stars are beautiful. There seems to be someone else in the field running too. Sweetback dives down and the other shadow disappears too. Sweetback takes out a knife. It's a Mexican going the other way through the grass but they never meet . . . After a while Sweetback stands up and begins to run again.

DAY A deputy driving down a country road he thinks he sees something moving in the gully. The car does a U-turn and drives back slowly. Then the car does another U-turn and resumes its original direction.

DAY Barking dogs behind a steel fence. The car that did the U-turn pulls up to the house and the deputy leaps out and bangs on the door. He and another guy run from the house to the kennels. The deputy and the guy run to the car with three vicious looking dogs in tow on guard leashes, they hop in the car.

TWILIGHT Sweetback running. The sound of barking in the distance. The two men and the dogs are running . . . The trail is fresh and the dogs follow it with swift deadly accuracy.

NIGHT Sweetback running.

NIGHT "He gonna make it . . . he's gonna get there before we do," the man says.

"Goddam dogs." Deputy explodes.

"Dogs moving faster than we are."

"Just get a glimpse of his black ass if the moon comes up and he's dead."

"He's farther ahead than that."

"Let the dogs go!"

"What!"

"Let 'em go . . . they got four legs he's only got two," the deputy orders.

"They'd tear him apart . . . I won't do it!"

"Let 'em go!! Goddamit."

The deputy and the man begin to struggle . . . one of the dogs breaks loose and shoots off, his leash trailing behind him. They fall and roll over and another dog breaks away . . . Finally they stop struggling.

"Sorry but I just couldn't let him get away," the deputy says. He puts out his hand to shake, "no hard feelings."

"Well, I guess what's done is done save some taxpayers money," he pats the last dog. They laugh.

"Listen . . . no barking," the deputy says.

"Yep" . . . the man nods. "Well, ain't no need for you to miss the fun Rinny," and he unfastens the last dog.

The deputy and the man sigh and wave their arms to get back their circulation and then they sit down.

FIRST DAWN A wide calm river. Rinny is standing on the bank whimpering he dips his head in the water and drinks . . . the water is bloody. An enormous close up of an eye . . . the eye is half under water . . . the camera pulls back and we see the eye belongs to the body of a dog . . .

a little further off the body of another dead dog is floating . . . the camera pans to the opposite bank and up to the hills in the distance . . . and instead of The End the words MORAL comes on the screen followed by a card saying *A BAD ASS NIGGER IS GONNA BE COMING BACK TO COLLECT SOME DUES*

DIALOGUE

(SWEETBACK LOSING HIS CHERRY TITLE SEQUENCE)

WHORE:
Come here. Close the door. Close the door . . . You, ain't at the photographer's. You ain't gettin' your picture taken . . . Move . . . (Moans) Oh, God. (Screams . . . Moans) Oh, son. Oh, you got a sweet, you got a sweet, sweetback. Oh, that's hot . . . Oh, God. Oh, God. Oh, son, you, son.

(BROTHEL CIRCUS SCENE INCLUDING BEATLE'S FIRST DIALOGUE WITH COPS)

DETECTIVE #1:
Besides, we're getting a lot of static from the commissioner about that stiff we found yesterday, you know what I mean?

BEATLE:
We don't know nothin' about no dead man.

DETECTIVE #2:
We know that but the commissioner doesn't. We just want to borrow one of your boys for a couple

of hours and take him downtown to make us look
good officialwise.

BEATLE:

Why me? I'm short one man already. George is
sick . . .

DETECTIVE #2:

You're our friend. We knew you'd be willing to lend
a hand.

BEATLE:

When did you people start getting so interested in
black folks . . . dead or alive?

DETECTIVE #1:

Progress.

BEATLE:

I can't, I'm short . . . I only got two guys working
now . . . Donald to explain, Sweetback to train, and
the two of 'em to trounce and bounce.

DETECTIVE #2:

We got a nice understanding, Beatle.

BEATLE:

It's mutual. Everybody profits.

DETECTIVE #2:

Let's keep it that way.

GOOD DYKE FAIRY GODMOTHER:

I'm the Good Dyke Fairy Godmother. Yes, the Good Dyke Fairy Godmother. Why didn't you know that all good dykes have fairy godmothers? And I'm here to answer this prayer of a good dyke. Yes, the Good Dyke Fairy Godmother. Didn't you know that all good dykes have fairy godmothers? And I'm here to answer the prayers of a good dyke. Zap, child.

(Crowd giggles and screeches.)

BEATLE:

Why me, I'm short-handed as it is . . . George is sick.

CROWD:

Come on baby, Sweetback.

Come on girl.

Clean on down to the bone.

Do it, do it do it.

You got it, Sweetback,

You got it brother.

You cool, Sweetback.

Different strokes for different folks.

Jelly, jelly, jelly.

(Screams)

DETECTIVE #1:

Which one of the boys? . . . We'll have him back for you before tomorrow noon.

GDFGM:

Ah ha. Now Sweetback here's the greatest, greatest in the world. Oh, I know what the hell you're thinking. Ha. How many times have I heard that before? Well as a special added attraction, if one of you young ladies would like to step up and try this gentleman, I'm sure you'll find him more than lively.

But, ah, that is to say, however, this offer is only open to, ah, sisters.

(Crowd laughs.)

DETECTIVE #2:

Ounce of protection . . . worth a pound of sniffin' around.

GDFGM:

That's all, folks.

BEATLE:

When Sweetback gets dressed, tell him I want to see him. Go with these gentlemen for the evening. See you tomorrow.

(OUTSIDE BROTHEL)

DETECTIVE #2:

Hell of a show you guys put on.

DETECTIVE #1:

We aren't going to use the handcuffs.

DETECTIVE #2:

Just like we told Beatle. Just a little eye-wash.

(IN THE PATROL CAR)

DETECTIVE #1:

Cigarette.

RADIO:

Calling W2, calling W2.

DETECTIVE #1:

Read you loud and clear.

RADIO:

Proceed to Unit 1. Crenshaw, Sector-2. Back up ten, W4 community disturbance possible 415 developing.

DETECTIVE #2:

Step on it.

DETECTIVE #1:

Roger.

(STREET NEAR RIOT)

DETECTIVE #1:

I got the cuffs . . . it's just for appearance sake. We
don't want anyone to come around here and find
you just sitting here.

DETECTIVE #2:

Don't go away.

CROWD:

Take your hands off him, jive police, jive police.
How would you like somebody coming into your
neighborhood?

DETECTIVE #3:

Come on, let's get him out of here before a crowd
forms.

(Crowd yells etc., in background.)

(PATROL CAR)

DETECTIVE #1:

You been stirring up the natives, kid?

DETECTIVE #2:

Nice night.

DETECTIVE #1:

Yeah.

DETECTIVE #2:

Nice night for a drive.

DETECTIVE #1:

A little walk too, maybe.

(OIL FIELDS)

DETECTIVE #1:

All right, why don't you step out over here. Get some fresh air. OK, that's better. OK, here . . . He doesn't look very tough to me, does he look tough to you?

DETECTIVE #2:

Naw, not too tough. Be careful. Don't mark his face.

DETECTIVE #1:

Oh no, all right.

DETECTIVE #2:

Stay on your feet. You're a tough man.

DETECTIVE #1:

Hey, wait a minute. Hey, Sweetback. Sorry, man. Forgot that you two attached together. Let's see if we can't get a little air between ya. There. You step over there. That's better, isn't it?

Let's see this militant. You don't look too tough now. If you stayed home at night, you wouldn't get into all this trouble, would you . . . What's the matter with you, you drunk?

DETECTIVE #2:

He looks like a sniper to me.

(Moo-Moo groans.)

MOO-MOO:

Thanks, man. Where we goin'?

SWEETBACK:

Where'd you get that "we" shit?

(BEATLES BATHROOM IN BROTHEL)

BEATLE:

Sweetback. Yeah. Where you gonna stay, baby? Yeah. We gotta chop a skoch. You know. Oh, lay it on me, hmmm Sweetback, baby, oh yeah. Looking good. Well, yeah, baby, you gonna have to be awful cool. Cause what you do reflects on all the rest of our little employees. We can't have that cause we got a good operation goin' here. Being in public relations, a nice little business. Yeah, man. But you don't have to worry about nothin'. I'm Beatle, me, Beatle, I'm your man. Everybody got a man. I'm your man. You know how the game go. Don't worry about a thing. Don't worry about it. That make you feel like a new one, baby. A brand new one. Yeah. But you know what now? Like you gonna kinda have to lay out, stretch out a little while, be real cool. Kinda lay dead. 01' Beatle let you know what's happenin', what's goin' down. Don't worry about nothin'. Just let me handle everything. Brother, just keep the faith. Beatle, ol' Beatle goin' to bring you through, cause this is just a skirmish. Ain't nobody scared, baby. But you keep the faith in me and you my man. You my favorite man. Can you dig it, baby? Together, you know, maintain. They can't bother you as long as Beatle's with you. Now you go on and hibernate like that 'ol bear and don't go nowhere, you dig it. Yeah, hah, mellow. Go cut the back door, now. Speed along and don't let nobody know where you at. Let sleeping dogs rest. You dig it, baby? Ha, ha, yeah.

(OUTSIDE BROTHEL)

COP #1:
You were in the car.

COP #2:
Were you still in the car, Sweetback?

COP #1:
How many men were in the ambush?

COP #2:
How'd they work it?

COP #1:
You know they're still unconscious.

COP #2:
Come on, they were your friends too.

COP #1:

You know where Moo-Moo might be?

COP #2:

We can't figure out what they used to beat them with.

COP:

Here, give me your coat.

(COMMISSIONER'S OFFICE AND PATROL CAR)

COMMISSIONER:

Humm.

COP #2:

Sir, I think we discovered the weapon and one of the assailants.

COMMISSIONER:

Uhhuh.

COP #2:

The suspect is a Mr. Sweetback.

COMMISSIONER:

Yeah.

COP #2:

I think we have a new development in the case.

GIRL:

Wash your car, mister?

COP #2:

Stop bothering me, now get away from here . . . I'm sorry sir.

COMMISSIONER:

Proceed.

GIRL:

No charge if you don't like it.

BOY:

Yeah, no charge if you don't like it.

COP #2:

Now just move away from the car.

COMMISSIONER:

Oh yes, I see, you have the witness called Sweetback, and Mr. Sweetback knows the whereabouts of the suspect, but that Mr. Sweetback has been injured in a fall. Not too badly, I hope.

COP #2:

Fell down and bruised himself, sir?

REPORTER:

Can we print that, Commissioner?

COMMISSIONER:

Of course. I have no secrets from the press.

COP #2:

I don't??

COMMISSIONER:

Fine, fine . . . You say the witness has given you the whereabouts of the suspect. Too bad the witness has injured himself in a fall.

COP #2:

OK . . . right, sir!

COMMISSIONER:

Proceed.

(OUTSIDE BROTHEL)

COP #1:

Well.

COP #2:

Commissioner says beat the information out of the nigger before we get him to the station.

COP #1:

Let's take him some place where we can really work on him.

(COMMISSIONER'S OFFICE)

TWO SIMULTANEOUS RADIOS:

The suspect twelve units has escaped have been alerted from the arresting search pattern has been constructed over the area Unit 6A-2 following barricades have been set up an explosion detonated immediately adjoining the streets vehicles causing extensive damage four additional units are now on the scene assisting when second officer went to the rescue of the driver all other available units are being deployed in searching the area the witness disappeared in the busy crowd impossible to escape apprehension matter of moments . . .

(WOMEN'S KITCHENETTE)

WOMAN:

You sure are jive and don't you tell me you came here looking for Steve. You know Steve's not here. He's got two more months to do . . . What are you, some kind of Indian Giver or something? You gave me to him . . . I knew you'd be back.

What do you want me to do, take them off? . . . Beg . . .

SWEETBACK:

No.

WOMAN:

You too proud to beg?

SWEETBACK:

No, but you wouldn't take them off if I did.

WOMAN:

You know every Goddamn thing, don't you . . .
Well, first things first.

VOICE:

Where's Sweetback?

VOICE #2:

Where's Sweetback?

(BEATLE'S ROOM)

BEATLE:

I don't know where Sweetback is.

DETECTIVE #3:

Where is Sweetback?

BEATLE:

I don't know where Sweetback is.

DETECTIVE #4:

Come on, come on, you can tell us.

BEATLE:

I don't know where Sweetback is.

DETECTIVE #3:

He seems to be hard of hearing.

DETECTIVE #4:
If he don't talk, he's going to be.

DETECTIVE #3:
Where's Sweetback? Where is he?

DETECTIVE #4:
Where's Sweetback?

BEATLE:
I don't know where Sweetback is.

DETECTIVE #3:
Where's Sweetback?

DETECTIVE #4:
Come on, boy.

(SHOT)

DETECTIVE #4:
Look at me.

BEATLE:
I don't know where Sweetback is.

DETECTIVE #4:
Come on, boy, talk.

DETECTIVE #3:
Where's Sweetback?

DETECTIVE #4:

Where's Sweetback?

DETECTIVE #3:

Where's Sweetback?

DETECTIVE #4:

He must be deaf.

DETECTIVE #3:

If he isn't, he's going to be.

DETECTIVE #4:

Look at me.

BEATLE:

I don't know where he is.

DETECTIVE #3:

Where's Sweetback?

BEATLE:

I don't know where he is.

DETECTIVE #4:

Where's Sweetback?

BEATLE:

I don't know where he is.

DETECTIVE #3:

Where's Sweetback?

BEATLE:

I don't know where he is.

DETECTIVE #4:

You only got one good ear left, boy, you want to save it? You want to save it? You want to talk?

(SHOT)

VOICE #1:

This guy's tough. Both ears are gone and he still won't talk.

VOICE #2:

Yeah, tough.

(CHURCH AND SWEETBACK IN HALLWAY)

WOMEN:

Oh, Jesus, wailing and crying . . .
Oh, Lord.
Oh, Jesus
Oh, Jesus.
Oh, Jesus, take him into glory, Lord.
Yes, Lord.
You know his heart.
Lord.
Oh, Jesus.

PREACHER:

Yes, Lord, black misery.

WOMEN:

Save him, save him, Lord.

You know his heart.

Save him.

Save him.

PREACHER:

Yes, Lord! Brothers and sisters, one of us. Brothers and sisters, we're here 'cause one of our brothers is in that box, but he's not dead. He's alive and with us.

WOMEN:

Jesus.

PREACHER:

We can't see him but we know he's here . . . I'm glad to tell you today that though he may be in that box he's gonna be in heaven with us. I can see him now . . . Good God Almighty, that's our man. Yes, my children, he is dead but he is not dead, he is with us here today.

WOMEN:

You know his heart.

PREACHER:

Our brother died of an overdose, an overdose of black misery . . . Yes, Lord! We'll bow our heads in prayer . . . What are you doing here, Sweetback? They're looking for you. You're about as hot as little sis's twat. Where you goin"?

SWEETBACK:

I want you to cover for me . . . I'm goin' upstairs to the farm.

PREACHER:

To the farm? You can't hide there.

(FARM)

(*Girl screams and moans.*)

(BACK OF CHURCH)

PREACHER:

You can't hide there.

(CHURCH AND SWEETBACK IN HALLWAY)

PREACHER:

They know all about the farm, and not only yesterday, the unwed mothers . . . the girls I get you from upstairs. The Man knows about everything . . . Ain't it strange how when we die, how our folks like to rejoice.

That's it. The hype I'm layin' down to them people inside it ain't dangerous. I'm just selling them a little bit of happiness from Happyland. We're all goin' to die so, so what I want 'em to have is some peace . . . My job, to make them believe that they're going to get it better on the other side. It's my job. Moo-Moo, the boy you saved, and those other kids, they're layin' down the real religion. They got it.

You offer some pretty good news to me, slappin' up on some white cops. Yes, indeed. I'm gonna say a Black Ave Maria for you. Like the kids say, "later for waiting." You saved the plant that they were planning to nip in the bud. That's why the Man's down on you. That's why the Man's down on you. I'm still gonna say a Black Ave Maria for you.

(GAMBLING DEN)

RADIO:
Right on we go on KGFJ Soul Radio with Sandra Z, the new hit by Earth, Wind and Fire.

MANAGER:
What does a dead man need bread for? So they was whipping a brother, and how about the brothers you shipped and the sisters you slipped? Life is tough, baby. A real struggle, from the womb to the tomb. Every dollar. That adds up to a dollar and a dime. That's why all of us niggers is so far behind.

CARD PLAYER 1:
And Africa shall stretch forth her arms.

CARD PLAYER 2
Yeah, and bring back a bloody stump.

CARD PLAYER 3:
Viva Puerto Rico Libre! (Long live a free Puerto Rico!)

(Card players laugh)

MANAGER:

I haven't forgot you staked me, Sweetback. If I had the dough, I would lay it on you, but I don't have it. I wouldn't shuffle or shit you, baby. Wouldn't do it for nothin' You can't get out of this town on wings, wheels, or steel. I wouldn't shuffle or shit you, brother.

Like I said, what does a dead man need bread for?

(BUS STATION AND CAR RIDE TO COUNTRY)

VOICE:

Albuquerque, Wichita Falls, San Diego.

BIG HENRY:

Just like the rail station boss. Full of pigs.

SWEETBACK:

Stop!

MOO-MOO:

I'm Moo-Moo, brothers.

MANAGER:

You the guy who got my buddy in all this trouble.

BIG HENRY:

Yeah.

MOO-MOO:

Where we goin', brothers?

MANAGER:

This is the best that I can do for you on such short notice. Buy yourself a last supper . . . You're a dead man.

(ABANDONED POWER STATION—MOTORCYCLE GANG'S TURF)

MOTORCYCLE GUY #1:

What have we here?

MOTORCYCLE GUY #2:

Looks like we have a couple of private trespassers and you just trespassed on private property.

MOTORCYCLE GUY #1:

That's a no no.

MOTORCYCLE GANG DOING THEIR NUMBER:

Let's kick their fucking ass, man.

They got to pay, man, they got to pay.

Give 'em a chance, man, this is a democracy.

Let's show 'em.

Hey, look at this, look at what he gave me.

Payment number one. Let's kick their fucking ass, man.

Yeah.

No, save them for something, something sporty.

Yeah, like what?

How about a duel?

A duel?

EVERYBODY:

A duel, a duel.

Sounds good to me.

Yeah, like in the good old days.

The good 'ol days.

Me, me and hairnet.

No, no, no. Got to throw him back. He's too little.

That's the one. (*Pointing at Sweetback*) I think we should have something good, really lay on something good.

ALL AT ONCE:

All right. The Pres. (*Laughter*) The Pres. All right, the Pres.

That'll be good.

Right on.

Yeah, when the Pres. comes back. Yeah, you gonna get it.

You and the Pres. are gonna duel.

Right on.

(*Shouts*)

The Pres., the Pres.

MOTORCYCLE GUY #1:

Hey Pres., have we got news for you . . . Hey, have we got work for you . . . We got a guy for you to duel . . . (*To Sweetback*) Your choice, man . . . What's it gonna be? . . . Name your weapons. Come on . . .

GANG:

Hey, how about knives?

MOTORCYCLE GUY #1

Go on, baby . . . Come on, man, what's it gonna be? Huh? What's it gonna be, man? Come on, man come on, babe, what's it gonna be? . . . Let's go huh, what's it gonna be? . . . Hey.

SWEETBACK:

Fucking.

(Gang shouts, indignant.)

PRES (BIG SADIE):

Shut up.

(Shouting, engines and clapping)

PRES:

Well, *(echo)*.

MOTORCYCLE GUY:

Bet Sambo's so scared he can't even get it on.

MOTORCYCLE GIRL:

After the Pres. does you in, then we'll do you in.

GANG:

YEAH.
Yeah.
Get it on.

Ball him in the bad health, Pres.
Do it to him, Pres.
Get it, Pres., get it.
(*Laughing, shouts, clapping*) Get it, Pres.

PRES:

OOOOOh, Sweetback, oooooh. (*screams*), Sweetback get it. Sweetback (*screams*), Sweetback (*giggles*).

MOTORCYCLE GUY:

Shit.

(OUTSIDE COUNTRY BAR-POOL HALL, BEFORE FIGHT)

MOTORCYCLE GUY #1:

You'll be cool here. We'll fix you up with help in the morning.

MOTORCYCLE GUY #2:

Nobody'll bother you here . . . Have a good time . . . Come on . . .

MOTORCYCLE GUY #3:

No danger here.

MOTORCYCLE GUY #1:

Did you get 'em on the phone?

MOTORCYCLE GUY #2:

Yeah, yeah.

MOTORCYCLE GUY #3:
How long will it take?

(OUTSIDE COUNTRY BAR-POOL HALL AFTER FIGHT)

BLACK MOTORCYCLE GUY:
Big Sadie heard her guy planning this cross . . . so she called us. Look here, I can only take one of you . . . I won't get ten feet with three people on this bike . . . They told me to pick up Sweetback . . . You Sweetback, ain't you?

SWEETBACK:
Take him.

BLACK MOTORCYCLE GUY:
You know what you're doin' man?

SWEETBACK:
He's our future, Brer. Take him.

MOO-MOO:
Sweetback. (*They shake hands.*)

(SWEETBACK RUNNING—COUNTRY NIGHT— AQUEDUCT DAY)

SWEETBACK'S HEAD:
come on feet
cruise for me

trouble ain't no place to be
come on feet
do your thing
come on feet
do your thing
you're on old whitey's game
come on legs
come on run
come on legs
come on run
guilty's what he say you done
come on knees
don't be mean
come on knees
don't be mean
ain't first red you ever seen
come on feet
do your thing
come on baby
don't cop out on me
come on baby
don't give in on me
come on feet
cruise for me
come on legs
come on run
come on feet
do your thing
who put the bad mouth on me
anyway the way I pick em up
and put em down

even if it got
my name on it
won't catch me now

(CONFERENCE ROOM AND COMMISSIONER'S OFFICE)

COMMISSIONER:

I want them, do you hear, and I want them now. God, there could be an uprising on our hands. Cop killers and niggers to boot. No patrol will be safe in their area . . . That's all.

Hey, Rossie, Bill, just a minute . . . Ah, YOU guys, I didn't mean any offense by, aah, by that word I used. It's a figure of speech, you understand. You know you guys could be a real credit to your people if you brought those guys in. OK?

(SWEETBACK RUNNING AND MOTEL RAID)

SWEETBACK'S HEAD:

come on feet
cruise for me
come on legs
come on run
come on feet
do your thing
lord you sure do get around
never put me in some cold-ass ground
sure is dark

never been out this way
mama anyway I'm safe and sound
bet I broke the Olympic 220
across country
or something
sure is lonely
sure most quietest turf I ever seen
what ever happened to the sun
sure gone away
sure blacker than a landlords soul
must have run all day
yeah must have run all day
sure am a bitch
must have run all day
sure yeah
yeah baby
come on feet
cruise for me
come on feet
come on run
come on legs
come on run
come on feet
do your thing
come on feet
do your thing

(MOTEL ROOM)

DETECTIVE #1:
That's not him.

COP:

So what.

(Man groans)

(SWEETBACK RUNNING—NIGHT—THROUGH CITY STREETS)

SWEETBACK'S HEAD:

come on feet
cruise for me
come on feet
come on run
come on legs
come on run
come on feet
do your thing
come on feet
do your thing

(COMMISSIONER'S OFFICE)

DETECTIVE #3:

Bingo, we got him.

(MORGUE)

COMMISSIONER:

If things change, the majority of people will decide where and when. This is a democracy, not communism. We're all going to respect the law or pay the consequences. As a citizen, you are required by law to aid us in this identification . . . Is this Sweetback's body?

BEATLE:

I ain't learned to read lips yet.

DONALD:

He lost his hearing. He ain't able to read lips yet.

(STREETS—LOOKING FOR SWEETBACK)

GHETTO FOLKS:

1. I told you one time I ain't seen Sweetback . . . Never heard of him . . . What else do he go by?
2. I'm positive I've never seen him . . .
3. Huh, yeah, thank you.
4. I've been looking for him myself
5. I don't know no Sweetback!
6. I ain't saw Sweetback.
7. I haven't seen him.

(WOMAN AT HOME WITH KIDS)

WOMAN:

I just keep these kids for the county and make these things for old people . . . Like this. Pretty, ain't they pretty? But when the kids get so grown and so bad they jest takes 'em away from me . . . I mighta had a Leroy once, but I don't rightly remember. They get so bad and so grown . . . I mighta had a Leroy once, but I don't remember . . . Just makes things for older people and keep kids for the county. Jest takes 'em away from me. I might have had a Leroy once, but I can't rightly remember. When the kids get bad and older, they usually take them away from me. I might have had a Leroy, but I don't . . . remember . . . When the kids get older and bad, they usually take them away from me . . . Just take them away from me and I mighta had a Leroy once, but I can't rightly remember . . .

(STREETS—POLICE QUESTIONING)

GHETTO FOLKS:

1. NO! Other people I don't give a damn about . . . I don't know nobody but my own Goddamn self . . .

(FUNKY NIGHTCLUB DRESSING ROOM)

SINGER:

No, I haven't seen Sweetback. I haven't seen him in a long time . . . Look, I never see the cat. If I never see him, it won't be too soon for me, you understand? You understand, man? . . . I haven't seen the cat and I don't want to see him. You just keep leaning and leaning and leaning, get the fuck off my back, man. I'm clean, man, look, I'm clean . . . There's nothing there, look, look. When I get pissed off, man, I will throw a natural-born nigger fit on you, understand, so why don't you leave . . . Why don't you leave. I am clean, look . . . Nothing, nothing. No place, man. I'm clean, so stop leaning on me. I ain't on the street no more, understand? I ain't in the trade no more. I just want to be left alone, baby. So don't push me. You're pushing my button, baby. You're pushing my button. Leave, split, leave, mother fucker.

Sweetback, man, shit!

(STAGE)

SINGER:
(*Laughing*) I love you, I love you, I love you.

(COMMISSIONER'S OFFICE)

COMMISSIONER:
Fuck the reporters! I know they're out there! 'Now look you guys, he's got one chance. Right here! Now lets get him.

(STREETS—POLICE QUESTIONING)

GHETTO FOLKS:
1. No, no, I haven't seem him. Sweetback? No, I haven't, I haven't seen him . . . Thank you, but I haven't seen him.
2. I haven't seen him.

(OUTSKIRTS OF CITY—SWEETBACK RUNNING),

CHORUS OF COLORED BOURGEOIS ANGELS:
they bled your Mama
they bled your Papa

SWEETBACK:
but they won't bleed me
nigger scared and pretend they don't see

COLORED ANGELS:
just like you Sweetback

SWEETBACK:
just like I used to be work your black behind to the
gums and you supposed to Thomas til he done

COLORED ANGELS:
you got to Thomas Sweetback
they bled your brother
they bled your sister

SWEETBACK:
yeah but he won't bleed me

(DESERT: COP AND GEEZER)

COP:
Alright, now why'd you run?

GEEZER:
Why'd I run?

COP:

Uh huh.

GEEZER:

I ran cause I gave my word I'd run.

COP:

Gave what word?

GEEZER:

I promised to run.

COP:

You promised who, what?

GEEZER:

This guy gave me five dollars to change duds with him. Told me if anybody come after me to just keep on running.

COP:

Was he a black guy?

GEEZER:

Yeah, . . . colored.

COP:

What'd he look like?

GEEZER:

Like a buddy I used to pal around with back in Denver.

COP:

Now would you say he was about this tall? Around this size?

GEEZER:

Yeah, about like that.

COP:

What was he doin'?

GEEZER:

Poorly.

COP:

You mean how he was doin'.

GEEZER:

Yeah, poorly.

(DESERT)

COLORED ANGELS:

By and by . . .
By and by . . .
progress Sweetback

SWEETBACK:

that's what he want you to believe

COLORED ANGELS:

No progress Sweetback

SWEETBACK:
he ain't stopped clubbing you for four hundred
years . . . And he don't intend to for a million

COLORED ANGELES.
he sure treat us bad Sweetback,

SWEETBACK:
we can make him do us better

COLORED ANGELS:
chicken ain't nothing but a bird
white man ain't nothing but a turd
nigger ain't shit
god's gonna trouble the water
wade in the water children
wade in the water children

SWEETBACK:
get my hand on a trigger

COLORED ANGELES:
you talking revolution Sweetback

SWEETBACK:
I want to get off these knees

COLORED ANGELS:
you talking revolution Sweetback

SWEETBACK:
somebody listen to me

COLORED ANGELS:

if he can't burn you out he'll stomp you out

SWEETBACK:

he won't waste me

COLORED ANGELS:

let it shine
let it shine
let it shine

he bopped your Mama
he bopped your Papa

SWEETBACK:

but he won't waste me

COLORED ANGELS:

you can't make it on wings, wheels, or steel
Sweetback

SWEETBACK:

we got feet

COLORED ANGELS:

you can't get away on wings, wheels, or steel Sweetback

SWEETBACK:

niggers got feet

COLORED ANGELES:

they bled your brother
they bled your sister

SWEETBACK:

your brother and your sister too . . . how come it took me so long to see . . . how he gets us to use each other . . .

COLORED ANGELS:

niggers scared

SWEETBACK:

we got to get it together . . . if he kick a brother it gotta be like he's kicking your mother

COLORED ANGELS:

he got your brother
don't let him get you
haul your black ass Sweetback
he ain't gonna let you stand tall Sweetback
the man knows everything Sweetback
the man knows everything

SWEETBACK:

then he oughta know I'm tired of him fucking with me!!

(SWEETBACK ON THE RUN—FIELDS)

COLORED ANGELS FINALLY GETTING IT TOGETHER AND ACTING BLACK:

run Sweetback
run mother fucker
they bled your sister

SWEETBACK:

they won't bleed me

BLACK ANGELS:

haul your black ass . . .
run mother fucker

(SWEETBACK ON THE RUN—TRUCK, MEXICANS)

MEXICANS:

Derecho, amigo . . . Mexico
Cuidado.

Mexico . . . straight ahead.
Vaya con Dios . . .

(SWEETBACK ON THE RUN—TRAIN)

BLACK ANGELS:

they bled your Mama
they bled your brother
they bled your sister

(LUNCH COUNTER)

GAY #1:

No, chile, I mean officer, I didn't see Mr. Sweetback.

GAY #2:

If you see him, send him here.

GAY #1:

I'm a militant queen.

GAY #3:

Won't I do, officer?

(SWEETBACK ON THE RUN)

VOICES:

1. Anybody can tell you that don't add up to a dollar, that, adds up to a dollar and a dime . . .
2. Stand up straight . . .
3. Buy yourself a last supper, you're a dead man . . .
4. Your choice, man . . . What's it gonna be, man . . .

BLACK ANGELS:

they bled your sister
they bled your brother

(ROCK CONCERT)

DEPUTY:

I thought I saw Sweetback.

SHERIFF:

Where?

DEPUTY:

Over there in the clump of bushes.

SHERIFF:

Are you sure?

DEPUTY:

If it ain't him, why was he goin' in the wrong direction?

(Both laugh)

(SWEETBACK ON THE RUN—DEPUTY AND DOG MAN ON HIS TRAIL)

TRAINER:

He's heading for the border. He's going to get there before we do. He's gonna get across the border before we catch him. He's gonna get there before we do.

SHERIFF:

Goddamn dogs.

TRAINER:

Dogs movin' faster than we are.

SHERIFF:

Just let me draw a bead on his black ass and he's dead.

TRAINER:

He's further ahead than that.

SHERIFF:

Just one Goddamn glimpse of his black ass and he's dead.

TRAINER:

He's gonna make it.

SHERIFF:

Let the dogs go.

TRAINER:

No, I won't do it.

SHERIFF:

Let the dogs go, damn it.

TRAINER:

I won't do it.

SHERIFF:

Let the dogs loose. They got four legs, we only got two.

TRAINER:

I won't do it, they'll tear him apart.

SHERIFF:

Turn loose of those dogs.

BLACK ANGELS:

they bled your Mama
they bled your Papa
they bled your brother

SHERIFF:

Sorry, no hard feelings, I just had to catch him.

TRAINER:

Well, what's done is done.

TRAINER:

I guess it'll save the taxpayers some money. (*Both laugh.*)

BLACK ANGELS:

they bled your sister

SHERIFF:

Listen, no barking.

TRAINER:

Yep.

I guess there's no sense of you hanging around here, Rinny. Ain't no need of you missing the fun, Rinny. Go on, boy . . .

(SIGN CARD)

A BAADASSSSS NIGGER IS COMING BACK TO COLLECT SOME DUES

CODAS

Attention: Mr. Jack Valenti,
          President

Gentlemen:

As you know I am the director and producer of the film entitled "SWEET SWEETBACK'S BAADASSSSS SONG". "SWEET SWEETBACK'S BAADASSSSS SONG" is a Black film. As a Black artist and independent producer of motion pictures, I refuse to submit this film, made from Black perspective for Blacks, to the Motion Picture Code and Administration for rating that would be applicable to the Black community. Neither will I "self apply" an "X" rating to my movie, if such a rating, is to be applicable to Black audiences, as called for by the Motion Pictures Code and Administration rules. I charge that your film rating body has no right to tell the Black community what it may or may not see. Should the rest of the community submit to your censorship that is its business, but White standards shall no longer be imposed on the Black community.

When an artist refuses to submit work to your jury (all White) your rules require him to self apply an "X" rating to his film. Such a rating necessarily limits the number of persons who will see the film and stigmatizes the film. This is intolerable to me as it should be to any other American. Therefore, I have decided to file suit against the Motion Picture Association and Mr. Jack Valenti, its president, on the basis that existing film rating practices violate state and federal anti-trust, unfair competition and other laws.

Rights of expression, the free flow of ideas, the nature of the creative process, and the rights of the Black community are at issue here. In my suit all appropriate judicial relief will be sought including money damages. The American Civil Liberties Union of Southern California will take an amicus curriae position in this suit particularly with respect to the unconstitutionality of the code as a form of prior censorship.

If a satisfactory reply is not made to this letter within ten days, I shall proceed.

Sincerely yours,
Melvin Van Peebles

CHRONOLOGY

Script finished, March 6, 1970, 6:20 P.M.
Shooting begun, May 11, 7:00 A.M.
Shooting finished, June 4, 8:15 P.M.
Editing begun, June 6, 6:00 A.M.
Images finished, October 9, 8:30 P.M.
Music recorded, October 21
Additional live sound (Foley Stage), November 11
Dubbing begun, November 16
Dubbing finished, November 20
November 24, 2:00 P.M., first composite print
January 12, 1971, 1:15 P.M., distribution deal closed, U.S. and Canada
February 1, midnight, album finished
March 8, record deal closed, Memphis
March 10, paid off first bread
March 31, smashed house record, Grand Circus Theatre, Detroit
April 2, smashed house record, Coronet Theatre, Atlanta

MELVIN VAN PEEBLES

WRITER—Books
Classified X—1998
Panther: A Novel—1995
Bold Money—1986
Just an Old Sweet Song—1976
The True American—1976
Don't Play Us Cheap—1972
Sweet Sweetback's Baadasssss Song—1971
Ain't Supposed to Die—1971
A Bear for the FBI—1968
Le Chinois de XIV—1966
The Big Heart—1957

DIRECTOR—Film
Le Conte du Ventre Plein—2000
Gang in Blue—1996
Vrooom Vroom Vrooom—1995
Identity Crisis—1989
Don't Play Us Cheap—1972
Sweet Sweetback's Baadasssss Song—1971
Watermelon Man—1970
The Story of a Three-Day Pass—1968
La Permission—1967
Cinq Cent Balles—1963
Sunlight—1957
Three Pickup Men for Herrick—1957

DIRECTOR—Theater
Champeen—1985
Waltz of the Stork—1981
Out There By Your Lonesome—1977
Don't Play Us Cheap—1973
Ain't Supposed to Die—1971

Composer—Film
Le Conte du Ventre Plein—2000
Vrooom Vroom Vrooom—1995
Don't Play Us Cheap—1973
Sweet Sweetback's Baadasssss Song—1971
Watermelon Man—1970
The Story of a Three-Day Pass—1968
Cinq Cent Balles—1963
Sunlight—1957
Three Pickup Men for Herrick—1957

Composer—Albums
Ghetto Gothic—1996
*What the #@!%. . . . You Mean I Can't
Sing?*—1978
Serious as a Heart Attack—1970
Ain't Supposed to Die—1969
Brer Soul—1968

Producer
Le Conte du Ventre Plein—2000
Classified X—1998
Gang in Blue—1996
Vrooom Vroom Vrooom—1995

Panther—1995
Identity Crisis—1989
Sweet Sweetback's Baadasssss Song—1971
Sunlight—1957
Three Pickup Men for Herrick—1957

ABOUT THE AUTHOR

Melvin Van Peebles has worked in every medium of the entertainment industry, from music (a three-time Grammy Award nominee) to television (an Emmy Award winner) to Broadway as a writer and director (eleven Tony Award nominations), and after thirty years his blockbuster movie, *Sweet Sweetback's Baadasssss Song*, remains on *Variety*'s list of all-time top grossing films. The film was recently released on DVD.

Mr. Van Peebles' works are taught at such distinguished schools as Yale, Harvard, and Columbia. Scott Gentry's book, *The Film 100*, recognized Mr. Van Peebles as one of the most influential people in the history of cinema for his commercialization of both independent and black films.

Mr. Van Peebles began his career as a ten-year-old selling second-hand clothes to winos. Since then, he has been involved with, among other things, the Boy Scouts, Astronomy, Youth for Christ, the Strategic Air Command, the Merchant Marine, the Artillery, the Post Office, Cable Cars, The Netherlands Comedie, the ACLU, the Cinematique Francaise, the Harkness Ballet, Boston Marathons, Pinochle, the Block, Blues, Dues, the Senegalese Police and the Mexican immigration authorities. Recently, Mr. Van Peebles was awarded the prestigious French Legion of Honor.

His book, *The Making of Sweet Sweetback's Baadasssss Song,* upon which his son Mario Van Peebles' movie *Baadasssss* is based and which serves as an excerpt from one of the volumes of his upcoming autobiography, is in its fourth U.S. printing. It has also been published in the U.K. and translated into French and Japanese.